FRANKENSTEIN

Mary Shelley

SPARK PUBLISHING

© 2002, 2007 by Spark Publishing, A Division of Barnes & Noble

This Spark Publishing edition 2014 by SparkNotes LLC, an Affiliate of Barnes & Noble

122 Fifth Avenue
New York, NY 10011
www.sparknotes.com

ISBN 978-1-4114-6954-9

Please submit changes or report errors to www.sparknotes.com/errors.

Printed in Canada

10 9 8 7 6

CONTENTS

CONTEXT

Did I request thee, Maker, from my clay
To mould me Man, did I solicit thee
From darkness to promote me?
(See QUOTATIONS, *p. 45)*

IN THE SUMMER OF 1816, a young, well-educated woman from England traveled with her lover to the Swiss Alps. Unseasonable rain kept them trapped inside their lodgings, where they entertained themselves by reading ghost stories. At the urging of renowned poet Lord Byron, a friend and neighbor, they set their own pens to paper, competing to see who could write the best ghost story. The young woman, Mary Wollstonecraft Godwin, took the prize, having composed a story creepy enough not only to take its place alongside the old German tales that she and her Alpine companions had been reading, but also to become a bestseller in her time and a Gothic classic that still resonates with readers almost two centuries later.

Mary Wollstonecraft Godwin was born on August 30, 1797, in London, of prime literary stock. Her mother, Mary Wollstonecraft, was the author of *A Vindication of the Rights of Woman,* a feminist tract encouraging women to think and act for themselves. Wollstonecraft died giving birth to Mary, leaving her daughter in the care of her husband, William Godwin, a member of a circle of radical thinkers in England that counted Thomas Paine and William Blake among its ranks. Mary's upbringing in this rarefied atmosphere exposed her at an early age to cutting-edge ideas, and it forged useful connections for her to such notables as Lord Byron.

Another of the literary types that Mary met as a teenager was Percy Bysshe Shelley, a dashing young poet. Sparks flew, and, in 1814, they ran away together for a tour of France, Switzerland, and Germany—Mary escaping her family and Percy his wife. At first blissful, their affair soon came under strain. Percy's relationship with Mary waxed and waned with the demands of his wife, Harriet; meanwhile, Mary busied herself with another man. Despite these distractions, the relationship endured and was eventually formalized under scandalous circumstances: Harriet, pregnant with

Percy's child, drowned herself in London in November of 1816; Mary and Percy were married weeks later.

The union between Mary and Percy was not only romantic but also literary. Percy edited Mary's manuscript for *Frankenstein* and is commonly supposed to have written the preface under her name. *Frankenstein* was published on January 1, 1818, and became an immediate bestseller. Unfortunately for Mary, this success was a single bright spot amid a series of tragedies. From 1815 to 1819, three of her four children died in infancy; in 1822, Percy drowned off the shore of Tuscany, leaving Mary a widow and single mother. Mary turned to her husband's poetry and prose, editing and publishing his *Posthumous Poems* in 1824 and his *Poetical Works and Letters* in 1839. She spent the rest of her time on her own writing, publishing *Valperga* in 1823, *The Last Man* in 1826, *The Fortunes of Perkin Warbeck* in 1830, *Lodore* in 1835, and *Falkner* in 1837. Serious illness plagued Mary, and she died in London in February 1851.

Plot Overview

I**N A SERIES OF LETTERS,** Robert Walton, the captain of a ship bound for the North Pole, recounts to his sister back in England the progress of his dangerous mission. Successful early on, the mission is soon interrupted by seas full of impassable ice. Trapped, Walton encounters Victor Frankenstein, who has been traveling by dog-drawn sledge across the ice and is weakened by the cold. Walton takes him aboard ship, helps nurse him back to health, and hears the fantastic tale of the monster that Frankenstein created.

Victor first describes his early life in Geneva. At the end of a blissful childhood spent in the company of Elizabeth Lavenza (his cousin in the 1818 edition, his adopted sister in the 1831 edition) and friend Henry Clerval, Victor enters the university of Ingolstadt to study natural philosophy and chemistry. There, he is consumed by the desire to discover the secret of life and, after several years of research, becomes convinced that he has found it.

Armed with the knowledge he has long been seeking, Victor spends months feverishly fashioning a creature out of old body parts. One climactic night, in the secrecy of his apartment, he brings his creation to life. When he looks at the monstrosity that he has created, however, the sight horrifies him. After a fitful night of sleep, interrupted by the specter of the monster looming over him, he runs into the streets, eventually wandering in remorse. Victor runs into Henry, who has come to study at the university, and he takes his friend back to his apartment. Though the monster is gone, Victor falls into a feverish illness.

Sickened by his horrific deed, Victor prepares to return to Geneva, to his family, and to health. Just before departing Ingolstadt, however, he receives a letter from his father informing him that his youngest brother, William, has been murdered. Grief-stricken, Victor hurries home. While passing through the woods where William was strangled, he catches sight of the monster and becomes convinced that the monster is his brother's murderer. Arriving in Geneva, Victor finds that Justine Moritz, a kind, gentle girl who had been adopted by the Frankenstein household, has been accused. She is tried, condemned, and executed, despite her assertions of innocence. Victor grows despondent, guilty with the knowledge that the monster he has created bears responsibility for the death of two innocent loved ones.

Hoping to ease his grief, Victor takes a vacation to the mountains. While he is alone one day, crossing an enormous glacier, the monster approaches him. The monster admits to the murder of William but begs for understanding. Lonely, shunned, and forlorn, he says that he struck out at William in a desperate attempt to injure Victor, his cruel creator. The monster begs Victor to create a mate for him, a monster equally grotesque to serve as his sole companion.

Victor refuses at first, horrified by the prospect of creating a second monster. The monster is eloquent and persuasive, however, and he eventually convinces Victor. After returning to Geneva, Victor heads for England, accompanied by Henry, to gather information for the creation of a female monster. Leaving Henry in Scotland, he secludes himself on a desolate island in the Orkneys and works reluctantly at repeating his first success. One night, struck by doubts about the morality of his actions, Victor glances out the window to see the monster glaring in at him with a frightening grin. Horrified by the possible consequences of his work, Victor destroys his new creation. The monster, enraged, vows revenge, swearing that he will be with Victor on Victor's wedding night.

Later that night, Victor takes a boat out onto a lake and dumps the remains of the second creature in the water. The wind picks up and prevents him from returning to the island. In the morning, he finds himself ashore near an unknown town. Upon landing, he is arrested and informed that he will be tried for a murder discovered the previous night. Victor denies any knowledge of the murder, but when shown the body, he is shocked to behold his friend Henry Clerval, with the mark of the monster's fingers on his neck. Victor falls ill, raving and feverish, and is kept in prison until his recovery, after which he is acquitted of the crime.

Shortly after returning to Geneva with his father, Victor marries Elizabeth. He fears the monster's warning and suspects that he will be murdered on his wedding night. To be cautious, he sends Elizabeth away to wait for him. While he awaits the monster, he hears Elizabeth scream and realizes that the monster had been hinting at killing his new bride, not himself. Victor returns home to his father, who dies of grief a short time later. Victor vows to devote the rest of his life to finding the monster and exacting his revenge, and he soon departs to begin his quest.

Victor tracks the monster ever northward into the ice. In a dog-sled chase, Victor almost catches up with the monster, but the sea beneath them swells and the ice breaks, leaving an unbridgeable gap between them. At this point, Walton encounters Victor, and the narrative catches up to the time of Walton's fourth letter to his sister.

Walton tells the remainder of the story in another series of letters to his sister. Victor, already ill when the two men meet, worsens and dies shortly thereafter. When Walton returns, several days later, to the room in which the body lies, he is startled to see the monster weeping over Victor. The monster tells Walton of his immense solitude, suffering, hatred, and remorse. He asserts that now that his creator has died, he too can end his suffering. The monster then departs for the northernmost ice to die.

CHARACTER LIST

Victor Frankenstein The doomed protagonist and narrator of the main portion of the story. Studying in Ingolstadt, Victor discovers the secret of life and creates an intelligent but grotesque monster, from whom he recoils in horror. Victor keeps his creation of the monster a secret, feeling increasingly guilty and ashamed as he realizes how helpless he is to prevent the monster from ruining his life and the lives of others.

The monster The eight-foot-tall, hideously ugly creation of Victor Frankenstein. Intelligent and sensitive, the monster attempts to integrate himself into human social patterns, but all who see him shun him. His feeling of abandonment compels him to seek revenge against his creator.

Robert Walton The Arctic seafarer whose letters open and close *Frankenstein*. Walton picks the bedraggled Victor Frankenstein up off the ice, helps nurse him back to health, and hears Victor's story. He records the incredible tale in a series of letters addressed to his sister, Margaret Saville, in England.

Alphonse Frankenstein Victor's father, very sympathetic toward his son. Alphonse consoles Victor in moments of pain and encourages him to remember the importance of family.

Elizabeth Lavenza An orphan, four to five years younger than Victor, whom the Frankensteins adopt. In the 1818 edition of the novel, Elizabeth is Victor's cousin, the child of Alphonse Frankenstein's sister. In the 1831 edition, Victor's mother rescues Elizabeth from a destitute peasant cottage in Italy. Elizabeth embodies the novel's motif of passive women, as she waits patiently for Victor's attention.

Henry Clerval Victor's boyhood friend, who nurses Victor back to health in Ingolstadt. After working unhappily for his father, Henry begins to follow in Victor's footsteps as a scientist. His cheerfulness counters Victor's moroseness.

William Frankenstein Victor's youngest brother and the darling of the Frankenstein family. The monster strangles William in the woods outside Geneva in order to hurt Victor for abandoning him. William's death deeply saddens Victor and burdens him with tremendous guilt about having created the monster.

Justine Moritz A young girl adopted into the Frankenstein household while Victor is growing up. Justine is blamed and executed for William's murder, which is actually committed by the monster.

Caroline Beaufort The daughter of Beaufort. After her father's death, Caroline is taken in by, and later marries, Alphonse Frankenstein. She dies of scarlet fever, which she contracts from Elizabeth, just before Victor leaves for Ingolstadt at age seventeen.

Beaufort A merchant and friend of Victor's father; the father of Caroline Beaufort.

Peasants A family of peasants, including a blind old man, De Lacey; his son and daughter, Felix and Agatha; and a foreign woman named Safie. The monster learns how to speak and interact by observing them. When he reveals himself to them, hoping for friendship, they beat him and chase him away.

M. Waldman The professor of chemistry who sparks Victor's interest in science. He dismisses the alchemists' conclusions as unfounded but sympathizes with Victor's interest in a science that can explain the "big questions," such as the origin of life.

M. Krempe A professor of natural philosophy at Ingolstadt. He dismisses Victor's study of the alchemists as wasted time and encourages him to begin his studies anew.

Mr. Kirwin The magistrate who accuses Victor of Henry's murder.

CHARACTER LIST

ANALYSIS OF MAJOR
CHARACTERS

VICTOR FRANKENSTEIN

Victor Frankenstein's life story is at the heart of *Frankenstein*. A young Swiss boy, he grows up in Geneva reading the works of the ancient and outdated alchemists, a background that serves him ill when he attends university at Ingolstadt. There he learns about modern science and, within a few years, masters all that his professors have to teach him. He becomes fascinated with the "secret of life," discovers it, and brings a hideous monster to life. The monster proceeds to kill Victor's youngest brother, best friend, and wife; he also indirectly causes the deaths of two other innocents, including Victor's father. Though torn by remorse, shame, and guilt, Victor refuses to admit to anyone the horror of what he has created, even as he sees the ramifications of his creative act spiraling out of control.

Victor changes over the course of the novel from an innocent youth fascinated by the prospects of science into a disillusioned, guilt-ridden man determined to destroy the fruits of his arrogant scientific endeavor. Whether as a result of his desire to attain the god-like power of creating new life or his avoidance of the public arenas in which science is usually conducted, Victor is doomed by a lack of humanness. He cuts himself off from the world and eventually commits himself entirely to an animalistic obsession with revenging himself upon the monster.

At the end of the novel, having chased his creation ever northward, Victor relates his story to Robert Walton and then dies. With its multiple narrators and, hence, multiple perspectives, the novel leaves the reader with contrasting interpretations of Victor: classic mad scientist, transgressing all boundaries without concern, or brave adventurer into unknown scientific lands, not to be held responsible for the consequences of his explorations.

THE MONSTER

The monster is Victor Frankenstein's creation, assembled from old body parts and strange chemicals, animated by a mysterious spark. He enters life eight feet tall and enormously strong but with the mind of a newborn. Abandoned by his creator and confused, he tries to integrate himself into society, only to be shunned universally. Looking in the mirror, he realizes his physical grotesqueness, an aspect of his persona that blinds society to his initially gentle, kind nature. Seeking revenge on his creator, he kills Victor's younger brother. After Victor destroys his work on the female monster meant to ease the monster's solitude, the monster murders Victor's best friend and then his new wife.

While Victor feels unmitigated hatred for his creation, the monster shows that he is not a purely evil being. The monster's eloquent narration of events (as provided by Victor) reveals his remarkable sensitivity and benevolence. He assists a group of poor peasants and saves a girl from drowning, but because of his outward appearance, he is rewarded only with beatings and disgust. Torn between vengefulness and compassion, the monster ends up lonely and tormented by remorse. Even the death of his creator-turned-would-be-destroyer offers only bittersweet relief: joy because Victor has caused him so much suffering, sadness because Victor is the only person with whom he has had any sort of relationship.

Robert Walton

Walton's letters to his sister form a frame around the main narrative, Victor Frankenstein's tragic story. Walton captains a North Pole–bound ship that gets trapped between sheets of ice. While waiting for the ice to thaw, he and his crew pick up Victor, weak and emaciated from his long chase after the monster. Victor recovers somewhat, tells Walton the story of his life, and then dies. Walton laments the death of a man with whom he felt a strong, meaningful friendship beginning to form.

Walton functions as the conduit through which the reader hears the story of Victor and his monster. However, he also plays a role that parallels Victor's in many ways. Like Victor, Walton is an explorer, chasing after that "country of eternal light"—unpossessed knowledge. Victor's influence on him is paradoxical: one moment he exhorts Walton's almost-mutinous men to stay the path courageously, regardless of danger; the next, he serves as an abject example of the dangers of heedless scientific ambition. In his ultimate decision to terminate his treacherous pursuit, Walton serves as a foil (someone whose traits or actions contrast with, and thereby highlight, those of another character) to Victor, either not obsessive enough to risk almost-certain death or not courageous enough to allow his passion to drive him.

Themes, Motifs & Symbols

Themes

Themes are the fundamental and often universal ideas explored in a literary work.

Dangerous Knowledge

The pursuit of knowledge is at the heart of *Frankenstein*, as Victor attempts to surge beyond accepted human limits and access the secret of life. Likewise, Robert Walton attempts to surpass previous human explorations by endeavoring to reach the North Pole. This ruthless pursuit of knowledge, of the light (see "Light and Fire"), proves dangerous, as Victor's act of creation eventually results in the destruction of everyone dear to him, and Walton finds himself perilously trapped between sheets of ice. Whereas Victor's obsessive hatred of the monster drives him to his death, Walton ultimately pulls back from his treacherous mission, having learned from Victor's example how destructive the thirst for knowledge can be.

Sublime Nature

The sublime natural world, embraced by Romanticism (late eighteenth century to mid-nineteenth century) as a source of unrestrained emotional experience for the individual, initially offers characters the possibility of spiritual renewal. Mired in depression and remorse after the deaths of William and Justine, for which he feels responsible, Victor heads to the mountains to lift his spirits. Likewise, after a hellish winter of cold and abandonment, the monster feels his heart lighten as spring arrives. The influence of nature on mood is evident throughout the novel, but for Victor, the natural world's power to console him wanes when he realizes that the monster will haunt him no matter where he goes. By the end, as Victor chases the monster obsessively, nature, in the form of the Arctic desert, functions simply as the symbolic backdrop for his primal struggle against the monster.

THEMES

MONSTROSITY

Obviously, this theme pervades the entire novel, as the monster lies at the center of the action. Eight feet tall and hideously ugly, the monster is rejected by society. However, his monstrosity results not only from his grotesque appearance but also from the unnatural manner of his creation, which involves the secretive animation of a mix of stolen body parts and strange chemicals. He is a product not of collaborative scientific effort but of dark, supernatural workings.

The monster is only the most literal of a number of monstrous entities in the novel, including the knowledge that Victor used to create the monster (see "Dangerous Knowledge"). One can argue that Victor himself is a kind of monster, as his ambition, secrecy, and selfishness alienate him from human society. Ordinary on the outside, he may be the true "monster" inside, as he is eventually consumed by an obsessive hatred of his creation. Finally, many critics have described the novel itself as monstrous, a stitched-together combination of different voices, texts, and tenses (see TEXTS).

SECRECY

Victor conceives of science as a mystery to be probed; its secrets, once discovered, must be jealously guarded. He considers M. Krempe, the natural philosopher he meets at Ingolstadt, a model scientist: "an uncouth man, but deeply imbued in the secrets of his science." Victor's entire obsession with creating life is shrouded in secrecy, and his obsession with destroying the monster remains equally secret until Walton hears his tale.

Whereas Victor continues in his secrecy out of shame and guilt, the monster is forced into seclusion by his grotesque appearance. Walton serves as the final confessor for both, and their tragic relationship becomes immortalized in Walton's letters. In confessing all just before he dies, Victor escapes the stifling secrecy that has ruined his life; likewise, the monster takes advantage of Walton's presence to forge a human connection, hoping desperately that at last someone will understand, and empathize with, his miserable existence.

TEXTS

Frankenstein is overflowing with texts: letters, notes, journals, inscriptions, and books fill the novel, sometimes nestled inside each other, other times simply alluded to or quoted. Walton's letters envelop the entire tale; Victor's story fits inside Walton's letters; the monster's story fits inside Victor's; and the love story of Felix and Safie and references to *Paradise Lost* fit inside the monster's story. This profusion of texts is an important aspect of the narrative structure, as the various writings serve as concrete manifestations of characters' attitudes and emotions.

Language plays an enormous role in the monster's development. By hearing and watching the peasants, the monster learns to speak and read, which enables him to understand the manner of his creation, as described in Victor's journal. He later leaves notes for Victor along the chase into the northern ice, inscribing words in trees and on rocks, turning nature itself into a writing surface.

Motifs

Motifs are recurring structures, contrasts, and literary devices that can help to develop and inform the text's major themes.

Passive Women

For a novel written by the daughter of an important feminist, *Frankenstein* is strikingly devoid of strong female characters. The novel is littered with passive women who suffer calmly and then expire: Caroline Beaufort is a self-sacrificing mother who dies taking care of her adopted daughter; Justine is executed for murder, despite her innocence; the creation of the female monster is aborted by Victor because he fears being unable to control her actions once she is animated; Elizabeth waits, impatient but helpless, for Victor to return to her, and she is eventually murdered by the monster. One can argue that Shelley renders her female characters so passive and subjects them to such ill treatment in order to call attention to the obsessive and destructive behavior that Victor and the monster exhibit.

Abortion

The motif of abortion recurs as both Victor and the monster express their sense of the monster's hideousness. About first seeing his creation, Victor says: "When I thought of him, I gnashed my teeth, my eyes became inflamed, and I ardently wished to extinguish that life which I had so thoughtlessly made." The monster feels a similar disgust for himself: "I, the miserable and the abandoned, am an abortion, to be spurned at, and kicked, and trampled on." Both lament the monster's existence and wish that Victor had never engaged in his act of creation.

The motif appears also in regard to Victor's other pursuits. When Victor destroys his work on a female monster, he literally aborts his act of creation, preventing the female monster from coming alive. Figurative abortion materializes in Victor's description of natural philosophy: "I at once gave up my former occupations; set down natural history and all its progeny as a deformed and abortive creation; and entertained the greatest disdain for a would-be science, which could never even step within the threshold of real knowledge." As with the monster, Victor becomes dissatisfied with natural philosophy and shuns it not only as unhelpful but also as intellectually grotesque.

SYMBOLS

Symbols are objects, characters, figures, and colors used to represent abstract ideas or concepts.

LIGHT AND FIRE

"What could not be expected in the country of eternal light?" asks Walton, displaying a faith in, and optimism about, science. In Frankenstein, light symbolizes knowledge, discovery, and enlightenment. The natural world is a place of dark secrets, hidden passages, and unknown mechanisms; the goal of the scientist is then to reach light. The dangerous and more powerful cousin of light is fire. The monster's first experience with a still-smoldering flame reveals the dual nature of fire: he discovers excitedly that it creates light in the darkness of the night, but also that it harms him when he touches it.

The presence of fire in the text also brings to mind the full title of Shelley's novel, *Frankenstein: or, The Modern Prometheus.* The Greek god Prometheus gave the knowledge of fire to humanity and was then severely punished for it. Victor, attempting to become a modern Prometheus, is certainly punished, but unlike fire, his "gift" to humanity—knowledge of the secret of life—remains a secret.

Summary & Analysis

Preface and Letters 1–4

Summary: Preface

> *I saw the pale student of unhallowed arts kneeling*
> *beside the thing he had put together.*
> *(See* quotations, *p. 45)*

Frankenstein opens with a preface, signed by Mary Shelley but commonly supposed to have been written by her husband, Percy Bysshe Shelley. It states that the novel was begun during a summer vacation in the Swiss Alps, when unseasonably rainy weather and nights spent reading German ghost stories inspired the author and her literary companions to engage in a ghost story writing contest, of which this work is the only completed product.

Summary: Letter 1

> *What may not be expected in a country of eternal light?*
> *(See* quotations, *p. 46)*

The novel itself begins with a series of letters from the explorer Robert Walton to his sister, Margaret Saville. Walton, a well-to-do Englishman with a passion for seafaring, is the captain of a ship headed on a dangerous voyage to the North Pole. In the first letter, he tells his sister of the preparations leading up to his departure and of the desire burning in him to accomplish "some great purpose"—discovering a northern passage to the Pacific, revealing the source of the Earth's magnetism, or simply setting foot on undiscovered territory.

Summary: Letters 2–3

In the second letter, Walton bemoans his lack of friends. He feels lonely and isolated, too sophisticated to find comfort in his ship-mates and too uneducated to find a sensitive soul with whom to share his dreams. He shows himself a Romantic, with his "love for the marvellous, a belief in the marvellous," which pushes him along the perilous, lonely pathway he has chosen. In the brief third letter, Walton tells his sister that his ship has set sail and that he has full confidence that he will achieve his aim.

SUMMARY: LETTER 4

In the fourth letter, the ship stalls between huge sheets of ice, and Walton and his men spot a sledge guided by a gigantic creature about half a mile away. The next morning, they encounter another sledge stranded on an ice floe. All but one of the dogs drawing the sledge is dead, and the man on the sledge—not the man seen the night before—is emaciated, weak, and starving. Despite his condition, the man refuses to board the ship until Walton tells him that it is heading north. The stranger spends two days recovering, nursed by the crew, before he can speak. The crew is burning with curiosity, but Walton, aware of the man's still-fragile state, prevents his men from burdening the stranger with questions. As time passes, Walton and the stranger become friends, and the stranger eventually consents to tell Walton his story. At the end of the fourth letter, Walton states that the visitor will commence his narrative the next day; Walton's framing narrative ends and the stranger's begins.

ANALYSIS: PREFACE AND LETTERS 1–4

The preface to *Frankenstein* sets up the novel as entertainment, but with a serious twist—a science fiction that nonetheless captures "the truth of the elementary principles of human nature." The works of Homer, Shakespeare, and Milton are held up as shining examples of the kind of work *Frankenstein* aspires to be. Incidentally, the reference to "Dr. Darwin" in the first sentence is not to the famous evolutionist Charles Darwin, who was seven years old at the time the novel was written, but to his grandfather, the biologist Erasmus Darwin.

In addition to setting the scene for the telling of the stranger's narrative, Walton's letters introduce an important character—Walton himself—whose story parallels Frankenstein's. The second letter introduces the idea of loss and loneliness, as Walton complains that he has no friends with whom to share his triumphs and failures, no sensitive ear to listen to his dreams and ambitions. Walton turns to the stranger as the friend he has always wanted; his search for companionship, and his attempt to find it in the stranger, parallels the monster's desire for a friend and mate later in the novel. This parallel between man and monster, still hidden in these early letters but increasingly clear as the novel progresses, suggests that the two may not be as different as they seem.

Another theme that Walton's letters introduce is the danger of knowledge. The stranger tells Walton, "You seek for knowledge and wisdom, as I once did; and I ardently hope that the gratification of your wishes may not be a serpent to sting you, as mine has been." The theme of destructive knowledge is developed throughout the novel as the tragic consequences of the stranger's obsessive search for understanding are revealed. Walton, like the stranger, is entranced by the opportunity to know what no one else knows, to delve into nature's secrets: "What may not be expected in a country of eternal light?" he asks.

Walton's is only the first of many voices in *Frankenstein*. His letters set up a frame narrative that encloses the main narrative—the stranger's—and provides the context in which it is told. Nested within the stranger's narrative are even more voices. The use of multiple frame narratives calls attention to the telling of the story, adding new layers of complexity to the already intricate relationship between author and reader: as the reader listens to Victor's story, so does Walton; as Walton listens, so does his sister. By focusing the reader's attention on narration, on the importance of the storyteller and his or her audience, Shelley may have been trying to link her novel to the oral tradition to which the ghost stories that inspired her tale belong. Within each framed narrative, the reader receives constant reminders of the presence of other authors and audiences, and of perspective shifts, as Victor breaks out of his narrative to address Walton directly and as Walton signs off each of his letters to his sister.

CHAPTERS 1–2

SUMMARY: CHAPTER 1

The stranger, who the reader soon learns is Victor Frankenstein, begins his narration. He starts with his family background, birth, and early childhood, telling Walton about his father, Alphonse, and his mother, Caroline. Alphonse became Caroline's protector when her father, Alphonse's longtime friend Beaufort, died in poverty. They married two years later, and Victor was born soon after.

Frankenstein then describes how his childhood companion, Elizabeth Lavenza, entered his family. At this point in the narrative, the original (1818) and revised (1831) versions of *Frankenstein* diverge. In the original version, Elizabeth is Victor's cousin, the daughter of Alphonse's sister; when Victor is four years old, Elizabeth's mother dies and Elizabeth is adopted into the Frankenstein family. In the revised version, Elizabeth is discovered by Caroline, on a trip to Italy, when Victor is about five years old. While visiting a poor

Italian family, Caroline notices a beautiful blonde girl among the dark-haired Italian children; upon discovering that Elizabeth is the orphaned daughter of a Milanese nobleman and a German woman and that the Italian family can barely afford to feed her, Caroline adopts Elizabeth and brings her back to Geneva. Victor's mother decides at the moment of the adoption that Elizabeth and Victor should someday marry.

SUMMARY: CHAPTER 2

Elizabeth and Victor grow up together as best friends. Victor's friendship with Henry Clerval, a schoolmate and only child, flourishes as well, and he spends his childhood happily surrounded by this close domestic circle. As a teenager, Victor becomes increasingly fascinated by the mysteries of the natural world. He chances upon a book by Cornelius Agrippa, a sixteenth-century scholar of the occult sciences, and becomes interested in natural philosophy. He studies the outdated findings of the alchemists Agrippa, Paracelsus, and Albertus Magnus with enthusiasm. He witnesses the destructive power of nature when, during a raging storm, lightning destroys a tree near his house. A modern natural philosopher accompanying the Frankenstein family explains to Victor the workings of electricity, making the ideas of the alchemists seem outdated and worthless. (In the 1818 version, a demonstration of electricity by his father convinces Victor of the alchemists' mistakenness.)

ANALYSIS: CHAPTERS 1–2

The picture that Victor draws of his childhood is an idyllic one. Though loss abounds—the poverty of Beaufort and the orphaning of Elizabeth, for instance—it is always quickly alleviated by the presence of a close, loving family. Nonetheless, the reader senses, even in these early passages, that the stability and comfort of family are about to be exploded. Shining through Victor's narration of a joyful childhood and an eccentric adolescence is a glimmer of the great tragedy that will soon overtake him.

Women in *Frankenstein* fit into few roles: the loving, sacrificial mother; the innocent, sensitive child; and the concerned, confused, abandoned lover. Throughout the novel, they are universally passive, rising only at the most extreme moments to demand action from the men around them. The language Victor uses to describe the relationship between his mother and father supports this image of women's passivity: in reference to his mother, he says that his father "came as a protecting spirit to the poor girl, who committed herself to his care." Elizabeth, Justine Moritz, and Caroline Beaufort all fit into this mold of the passive woman. Various metanarrative comments (i.e., remarks that pertain not to the content of the narrative but rather to the telling of the narrative) remind the reader of the fact that Victor's narrative is contained within Walton's. Victor interrupts his story to relate how Elizabeth became a part of his family, prefacing the digression with the comment, "But before I continue my narrative, I must record an incident." Such guiding statements structure Victor's narrative and remind the reader that Victor is telling his story to a specific audience—Walton.

Foreshadowing is ubiquitous in these chapters and, in fact, throughout the novel. Even Walton's letters prepare the way for the tragic events that Victor will recount. Victor constantly alludes to his imminent doom; for example, he calls his interest in natural philosophy "the genius that has regulated my fate" and "the fatal impulse that led to my ruin." Victor's narrative is rife with nostalgia for a happier time; he dwells on the fuzzy memories of his blissful childhood with Elizabeth, his father and mother, and Henry Clerval. But even in the midst of these tranquil childhood recollections, he cannot ignore the signs of the tragedy that lies in his imminent future; he sees that each event, such as the death of his mother, is nothing but "an omen, as it were, of [his] future misery."

This heavy use of foreshadowing has a dual effect. On the one hand, it adds to the suspense of the novel, leaving the reader wondering about the nature of the awful tragedy that has caused Victor so much grief. On the other hand, it drains away some of the suspense—the reader knows far ahead of time that Victor has no hope, that all is doomed. Words like "fate," "fatal," and "omen" reinforce the inevitability of Victor's tragedy, suggesting not only a sense of resignation but also, perhaps, an attempt by Victor to deny responsibility for his own misfortune. Describing his decision to study chemistry, he says, "Thus ended a day memorable to me; it decided my future destiny."

CHAPTERS 3–5

SUMMARY: CHAPTER 3

> *I will pioneer a new way, explore unknown powers, and
> unfold to the world the deepest mysteries of creation.*
> *(See* QUOTATIONS, *p. 45)*

At the age of seventeen, Victor leaves his family in Geneva to attend the university at Ingolstadt. Just before Victor departs, his mother catches scarlet fever from Elizabeth, whom she has been nursing back to health, and dies. On her deathbed, she begs Elizabeth and Victor to marry. Several weeks later, still grieving, Victor goes off to Ingolstadt.

Arriving at the university, he finds quarters in the town and sets up a meeting with a professor of natural philosophy, M. Krempe. Krempe tells Victor that all the time that Victor has spent studying the alchemists has been wasted, further souring Victor on the study of natural philosophy. He then attends a lecture in chemistry by a professor named Waldman. This lecture, along with a subsequent meeting with the professor, convinces Victor to pursue his studies in the sciences.

SUMMARY: CHAPTER 4

Victor attacks his studies with enthusiasm and, ignoring his social life and his family far away in Geneva, makes rapid progress. Fascinated by the mystery of the creation of life, he begins to study how the human body is built (anatomy) and how it falls apart (death and decay). After several years of tireless work, he masters all that his professors have to teach him, and he goes one step further: discovering the secret of life.

Privately, hidden away in his apartment where no one can see him work, he decides to begin the construction of an animate creature, envisioning the creation of a new race of wonderful beings. Zealously devoting himself to this labor, he neglects everything else—family, friends, studies, and social life—and grows increasingly pale, lonely, and obsessed.

SUMMARY: CHAPTER 5

One stormy night, after months of labor, Victor completes his creation. But when he brings it to life, its awful appearance horrifies him. He rushes to the next room and tries to sleep, but he is troubled by nightmares about Elizabeth and his mother's corpse. He wakes to discover the monster looming over his bed with a grotesque smile and rushes out of the house. He spends the night pacing in his courtyard. The next morning, he goes walking in the town of Ingolstadt, frantically avoiding a return to his now-haunted apartment.

As he walks by the town inn, Victor comes across his friend Henry Clerval, who has just arrived to begin studying at the university. Delighted to see Henry—a breath of fresh air and a reminder of his family after so many months of isolation and ill health—he brings him back to his apartment. Victor enters first and is relieved to find no sign of the monster. But, weakened by months of work and shock at the horrific being he has created, he immediately falls ill with a nervous fever that lasts several months. Henry nurses him back to health and, when Victor has recovered, gives him a letter from Elizabeth that had arrived during his illness.

ANALYSIS: CHAPTERS 3–5

Whereas the first two chapters give the reader a mere sense of impending doom, these chapters depict Victor irrevocably on the way to tragedy. The creation of the monster is a grotesque act, far removed from the triumph of scientific knowledge for which Victor had hoped. His nightmares reflect his horror at what he has done and also serve to foreshadow future events in the novel. The images of Elizabeth "livid with the hue of death" prepare the reader for Elizabeth's eventual death and connect it, however indirectly, to the creation of the monster.

Victor's pursuit of scientific knowledge reveals a great deal about his perceptions of science in general. He views science as the only true route to new knowledge: "In other studies you go as far as others have gone before you, and there is nothing more to know; but in scientific pursuit there is continual food for discovery and wonder." Walton's journey to the North Pole is likewise a search for "food for discovery and wonder," a step into the tantalizing, dark unknown.

The symbol of light, introduced in Walton's first letter ("What may not be expected in a country of eternal light?"), appears again in Victor's narrative, this time in a scientific context. "From the midst of this darkness," Victor says when describing his discovery of the secret of life, "a sudden light broke in upon me—a light so brilliant and wondrous." Light reveals, illuminates, clarifies; it is essential for seeing, and seeing is the way to knowledge. Just as light can illuminate, however, so can it blind; pleasantly warm at moderate levels, it ignites dangerous flames at higher ones. Immediately after his first metaphorical use of light as a symbol of knowledge, Victor retreats into secrecy and warns Walton of "how dangerous is the acquirement of knowledge." Thus, light is balanced always by fire, the promise of new discovery by the danger of unpredictable—and perhaps tragic—consequences.

The theme of secrecy manifests itself in these chapters, as Victor's studies draw him farther and farther away from those who love and advise him. He conducts his experiments alone, following the example of the ancient alchemists, who jealously guarded their secrets, and rejecting the openness of the new sciences. Victor displays an unhealthy obsession with all of his endeavors, and the labor of creating the monster takes its toll on him. It drags him into charnel houses in search of old body parts and, even more important, isolates him from the world of open social institutions. Though Henry's presence makes Victor become conscious of his gradual loss of touch with humanity, Victor is nonetheless unwilling to tell Henry anything about the monster. The theme of secrecy transforms itself, now linked to Victor's shame and regret for having ever hoped to create a new life.

Victor's reaction to his creation initiates a haunting theme that persists throughout the novel—the sense that the monster is inescapable, ever present, liable to appear at any moment and wreak havoc. When Victor arrives at his apartment with Henry, he opens the door "as children are accustomed to do when they expect a specter to stand in waiting for them on the other side," a seeming echo of the tension-filled German ghost stories read by Mary Shelley and her vacationing companions.

As in the first three chapters, Victor repeatedly addresses Walton, his immediate audience, reminding the reader of the frame narrative and of the multiple layers of storytellers and listeners. Structuring comments such as "I fear, my friend, that I shall render myself tedious by dwelling on these preliminary circumstances" both remind the reader of the target audience (Walton) and help indicate the relative importance of each passage.

Shelley employs other literary devices from time to time, including apostrophe, in which the speaker addresses an inanimate object, absent person, or abstract idea. Victor occasionally addresses some of the figures from his past as if they were with him on board Walton's ship. "Excellent friend!" he exclaims, referring to Henry. "How sincerely did you love me, and endeavor to elevate my mind, until it was on a level with your own." Apostrophe was a favorite of Mary Shelley's husband, Percy Bysshe Shelley, who used it often in his poetry; its occurrence here might reflect some degree of Percy's influence on Mary's writing.

CHAPTERS 6–8

SUMMARY: CHAPTER 6

Elizabeth's letter expresses her concern about Victor's illness and entreats him to write to his family in Geneva as soon as he can. She also tells him that Justine Moritz, a girl who used to live with the Frankenstein family, has returned to their house following her mother's death.

After Victor has recovered, he introduces Henry, who is studying Oriental languages, to the professors at the university. The task is painful, however, since the sight of any chemical instrument worsens Victor's symptoms; even speaking to his professors torments him. He decides to return to Geneva and awaits a letter from his father specifying the date of his departure. Meanwhile, he and Henry take a walking tour through the country, uplifting their spirits with the beauties of nature.

SUMMARY: CHAPTER 7

On their return to the university, Victor finds a letter from his father telling him that Victor's youngest brother, William, has been murdered. Saddened, shocked, and apprehensive, Victor departs immediately for Geneva. By the time he arrives, night has fallen and the gates of Geneva have been shut, so he spends the evening walking in the woods around the outskirts of the town. As he walks near the spot where his brother's body was found, he spies the monster lurking and becomes convinced that his creation is responsible for killing William. The next day, however, when he returns home, Victor learns that Justine has been accused of the murder. After the discovery of the body, a servant had found in Justine's pocket a picture of Caroline Frankenstein last seen in William's possession. Victor proclaims Justine's innocence, but the evidence against her seems irrefutable, and Victor refuses to explain himself for fear that he will be labeled insane.

SUMMARY: CHAPTER 8

Justine confesses to the crime, believing that she will thereby gain salvation, but tells Elizabeth and Victor that she is innocent—and miserable. They remain convinced of her innocence, but Justine is soon executed. Victor becomes consumed with guilt, knowing that the monster he created and the cloak of secrecy within which the creation took place have now caused the deaths of two members of his family.

ANALYSIS: CHAPTERS 6–8

Victor's incorporation of written letters into his story allows both Elizabeth and Alphonse to participate directly in the narrative, bypassing Victor to speak directly to Walton and the reader. However, at the same time that the letters increase the realism of the narrative, allowing the reader to hear the characters' distinct voices, they also make the overall narrative less plausible. It is unlikely that Frankenstein would remember the letters word-for-word and even more unlikely that Walton would record them as such in his own letters to his sister. Furthermore, there is the question of filtering: the recollections of either Victor or Walton, or both, could be biased, either subconsciously or consciously. The presence of these letters foregrounds the issue of whether or not the narrator is reliable.

Women continue to play a mostly passive role in the narrative. Although Elizabeth stands up for Justine's innocence, she, like Justine, is completely helpless to stop the execution. Only Victor has the power to do so, as he is in possession of crucial knowledge that could identify the real killer. It is clear where the power lies in the relationship between Victor and Elizabeth: he makes the decisions; she pleads with him to make the right ones.

Appearing in Ingolstadt at just the right moment to nurse Victor back to health, Henry serves as the line of communication between Victor and his family, presenting him with an avenue back to the warmth of society. In asking Victor to introduce him to the professors at the university, however, Henry drags him back into the realm of chemistry, science, and dangerous knowledge that he has just escaped. By accompanying Victor on his walking tour, Henry reawakens in him a sense of health, openness, and friendly society that he had lost during his months of work creating the monster. Henry plays the foil to Victor; he embodies relentless clarity, openness, concern, and good health, in sharp contrast to Victor's secrecy, self-absorption, and ill health.

CHAPTERS 9–10

SUMMARY: CHAPTER 9

After Justine's execution, Victor becomes increasingly melancholy. He considers suicide but restrains himself by thinking of Elizabeth and his father. Alphonse, hoping to cheer up his son, takes his children on an excursion to the family home at Belrive. From there, Victor wanders alone toward the valley of Chamounix. The beautiful scenery cheers him somewhat, but his respite from grief is short-lived.

Summary: Chapter 10

One rainy day, Victor wakes to find his old feelings of despair resurfacing. He decides to travel to the summit of Montanvert, hoping that the view of a pure, eternal, beautiful natural scene will revive his spirits.

When he reaches the glacier at the top, he is momentarily consoled by the sublime spectacle. As he crosses to the opposite side of the glacier, however, he spots a creature loping toward him at incredible speed. At closer range, he recognizes clearly the grotesque shape of the monster. He issues futile threats of attack to the monster, whose enormous strength and speed allow him to elude Victor easily. Victor curses him and tells him to go away, but the monster, speaking eloquently, persuades him to accompany him to a fire in a cave of ice. Inside the cave, the monster begins to narrate the events of his life.

Analysis: Chapters 9–10

These chapters contain some of the novel's most explicit instances of the theme of sublime nature, as nature's powerful influence on Victor becomes manifest. The natural world has noticeable effects on Victor's mood: he is moved and cheered in the presence of scenic beauty, and he is disconsolate in its absence. Just as nature can make him joyful, however, so can it remind him of his guilt, shame, and regret: "The rain depressed me; my old feelings recurred, and I was miserable." Shelley aligns Victor with the Romantic movement of late-eighteenth- to mid-nineteenth-century Europe, which emphasized a turn to nature for sublime experience—feelings of awe, hope, and ecstasy. Victor's affinity with nature is of particular significance because of the monster's ties to nature. Both distinctly at home in nature and unnatural almost by definition, the monster becomes a symbol of Victor's folly in trying to emulate the natural forces of creation.

Formerly a mysterious, grotesque, completely physical being, the monster now becomes a verbal, emotional, sensitive, almost human figure that communicates his past to Victor in eloquent and moving terms. This transformation is key to Victor's fuller understanding of his act of creation: before, it was the monster's physical strength, endurance, and apparent ill will that made him such a threat; now, it is his intellect. The monster clearly understands his position in the world, the tragedy of his existence and abandonment by his creator, and is out to seek either redress or revenge. For the first time, Victor starts to realize that what he has created is not merely the scientific product of an experiment in animated matter but an actual living being with needs and wants.

While Victor curses the monster as a demon, the monster responds to Victor's coarseness with surprising eloquence and sensitivity, proving himself an educated, emotional, exquisitely human being. While the monster's grotesque appearance lies only in the reader's imagination (and may be exaggerated by Victor's bias), his moving words stand as a concrete illustration of his delicate nature. For the reader, whose experience with the monster's ugliness is secondhand, it is easy to identify the human sensitivity within him and sympathize with his plight, especially in light of Victor's relentless contempt for him. The gap between the monster and Victor, and between the monster and human beings in general, is thus narrowed.

One of the ways in which the monster demonstrates his eloquence is by alluding to John Milton's *Paradise Lost,* one of the books he reads while living in the peasants' hovel (described later in the monster's narrative). The first of these allusions occurs in these chapters, when the monster tries to convince Victor to listen to his story. He entreats Victor to "remember, that I am thy creature: I ought to be thy Adam; but I am rather the fallen angel." By comparing Victor to God, the monster heaps responsibility for his evil actions upon Victor, scolding him for his neglectful failure to provide a nourishing environment.

CHAPTERS 11–12

SUMMARY: CHAPTER 11

Sitting by the fire in his hut, the monster tells Victor of the confusion that he experienced upon being created. He describes his flight from Victor's apartment into the wilderness and his gradual acclimation to the world through his discovery of the sensations of light, dark, hunger, thirst, and cold. According to his story, one day he finds a fire and is pleased at the warmth it creates, but he becomes dismayed when he burns himself on the hot embers. He realizes that he can keep the fire alive by adding wood, and that the fire is good not only for heat and warmth but also for making food more palatable.

In search of food, the monster finds a hut and enters it. His presence causes an old man inside to shriek and run away in fear. The monster proceeds to a village, where more people flee at the sight of him. As a result of these incidents, he resolves to stay away from humans. One night he takes refuge in a small hovel adjacent to a cottage. In the morning, he discovers that he can see into the cottage through a crack in the wall and observes that the occupants are a young man, a young woman, and an old man.

SUMMARY: CHAPTER 12

Observing his neighbors for an extended period of time, the monster notices that they often seem unhappy, though he is unsure why. He eventually realizes, however, that their despair results from their poverty, to which he has been contributing by surreptitiously stealing their food. Torn by his guilty conscience, he stops stealing their food and does what he can to reduce their hardship, gathering wood at night to leave at the door for their use.

The monster becomes aware that his neighbors are able to communicate with each other using strange sounds. Vowing to learn their language, he tries to match the sounds they make with the actions they perform. He acquires a basic knowledge of the language, including the names of the young man and woman, Felix and Agatha. He admires their graceful forms and is shocked by his ugliness when he catches sight of his reflection in a pool of water. He spends the whole winter in the hovel, unobserved and well protected from the elements, and grows increasingly affectionate toward his unwitting hosts.

ANALYSIS: CHAPTERS 11–12

The monster's growing understanding of the social significance of family is connected to his sense of otherness and solitude. The cottagers' devotion to each other underscores Victor's total abandonment of the monster; ironically, observing their kindness actually causes the monster to suffer, as he realizes how truly alone, and how far from being the recipient of such kindness, he is. This lack of interaction with others, in addition to his namelessness, compounds the monster's woeful lack of social identity.

The theme of nature's sublimity, of the connection between human moods and natural surroundings, resurfaces in the monster's childlike reaction to springtime. Nature proves as important to the monster as it is to Victor: as the temperature rises and the winter ice melts, the monster takes comfort in a suddenly green and blooming world, glorying in nature's creation when he cannot rejoice in his own. For a moment, he is able to forget his own ugliness and unnaturalness.

Like Victor, the monster comes to regard knowledge as dangerous, as it can have unforeseen negative consequences. After realizing that he is horribly different from human beings, the monster cries, "Of what a strange nature is knowledge! It clings to the mind, when it has once seized on it, like a lichen on the rock." Knowledge is permanent and irreversible; once gained, it cannot be dispossessed. Just as the monster, a product of knowledge, spins out of Victor's control, so too can knowledge itself, once uncovered, create irreversible harm.

Certain elements of the narrative style persist as the perspective transitions from Victor to the monster. Both narrators are emotional, sensitive, aware of nature's power, and concerned with the dangers of knowledge; both express themselves in an elegant, Romantic, slightly melodramatic tone. One can argue that the similarity of their tones arises as a function of the filtering inherent in the layered narrative: the monster speaks through Victor, Victor speaks through Walton, and Walton ultimately speaks through the sensitive, Romantic Shelley. However, one can also explore whether the structure of the novel itself helps explain these narrative parallels. The growing list of similarities between Victor and the monster suggests that the two characters may not be so different after all.

CHAPTERS 13–14

SUMMARY: CHAPTER 13

As winter thaws into spring, the monster notices that the cottagers, particularly Felix, seem unhappy. A beautiful woman in a dark dress and veil arrives at the cottage on horseback and asks to see Felix. Felix becomes ecstatic the moment he sees her. The woman, who does not speak the language of the cottagers, is named Safie. She moves into the cottage, and the mood of the household immediately brightens. As Safie learns the language of the cottagers, so does the monster. He also learns to read, and, since Felix uses Constantin-François de Volney's *Ruins of Empires* to instruct Safie, he learns a bit of world history in the process. Now able to speak and understand the language perfectly, the monster learns about human society by listening to the cottagers' conversations. Reflecting on his own situation, he realizes that he is deformed and alone. "Was I then a monster," he asks, "a blot upon the earth, from which all men fled, and whom all men disowned?" He also learns about the pleasures and obligations of the family and of human relations in general, which deepens the agony of his own isolation.

SUMMARY: CHAPTER 14

After some time, the monster's constant eavesdropping allows him to reconstruct the history of the cottagers. The old man, De Lacey, was once an affluent and successful citizen in Paris; his children,

Agatha and Felix, were well-respected members of the community. Safie's father, a Turk, was falsely accused of a crime and sentenced to death. Felix visited the Turk in prison and met his daughter, with whom he immediately fell in love. Safie sent Felix letters thanking him for his intention to help her father and recounting the circumstances of her plight (the monster tells Victor that he copied some of these letters and offers them as proof that his tale is true). The letters relate that Safie's mother was a Christian Arab who had been enslaved by the Turks before marrying her father. She inculcated in Safie an independence and intelligence that Islam prevented Turkish women from cultivating. Safie was eager to marry a European man and thereby escape the near-slavery that awaited her in Turkey. Felix successfully coordinated her father's escape from prison, but when the plot was discovered, Felix, Agatha, and De Lacey were exiled from France and stripped of their wealth. They then moved into the cottage in Germany upon which the monster has stumbled. Meanwhile, the Turk tried to force Safie to return to Constantinople with him, but she managed to escape with some money and the knowledge of Felix's whereabouts.

Analysis: Chapters 13–14

The subplot of Safie and the cottagers adds yet another set of voices to the novel. Their story is transmitted from the cottagers to the monster, from the monster to Victor, from Victor to Walton, and from Walton to his sister, at which point the reader finally gains access to it. This layering of stories within stories enables the reworking of familiar ideas in new contexts. One such idea is the sense of "otherness" that many characters in *Frankenstein* feel. The monster, whose solitude stems from being the only creature of his kind in existence and from being shunned by humanity, senses this quality of being different most powerfully. His deformity, his ability to survive extreme conditions, and the grotesque circumstances of his creation all serve to mark him as the ultimate outsider. Victor, too, is an outsider, as his awful secret separates him from friends, family, and the rest of society. In the subplot of the cottagers, this idea recurs in the figures of both Safie and her father. His otherness as a Muslim Turk in Paris results in a threat to his life from the prejudiced and figures in power. Her feelings of being oppressed by Islam's confining gender roles compel her to seek escape to the more egalitarian ideas of Christianity.

The monster's fascination with the relationship between Felix and Safie lies in his desperate desire for Victor to accept him. Felix's willingness to risk everything for the sake of someone who has been unjustly punished gives the monster hope that Victor will recognize the hurtful injustice of abandoning him. However, just as Felix's bravery in helping Safie's father escape stands in stark contrast to Victor's shameful unwillingness to save Justine, so does Felix's compassion for Safie underscore Victor's cold hatred for the monster.

Language and communication take center stage in these chapters, as the monster emerges from his infantile state and begins to understand and produce written and spoken language. His alienation from society, however, provides him no opportunity to communicate with others; rather, he is a one-way conduit, a voyeur, absorbing information from the cottagers without giving anything in return. The importance of language as a means of self-expression manifests itself in the monster's encounter with Victor on the glacier. Just as each distinct narrative voice contributes to the novel's richly woven web of allusions and biases, the monster's romanticization of the cottagers as kind and friendly reflects his desperate desire for companionship and affection.

Texts play an important role throughout the novel, especially in shaping the monster's conception of his identity and place in the world. As his language skills increase, the monster gains a sense of the world through Felix's reading of *Ruins of Empires*. In these chapters, he acquires the ability to understand the crucial texts that he soon discovers, including *Paradise Lost*. This text introduces him to Adam and Satan, to both of whom he eventually compares himself. In addition to shaping his identity, the written word provides the monster with a means of legitimizing his past. In offering to show Victor copies of Safie's letters, he hopes to validate his perspective on the tragedy that has befallen them and thus gain Victor's sympathy. His belief in the truth of the written word, however, seems particularly naïve in a novel with a narrative structure as complex as that of Frankenstein; just as he falsely assumes that *Paradise Lost* is historically accurate, he hopes groundlessly that his narrative can win Victor over.

One of the novel's persistent motifs is that of the passive woman, a gentle creature who submits to the demands of the active, powerful men around her. Safie turns this stereotype on its head when she boldly rejects her father's attempt to return her to the constraints and limitations of life in Constantinople. Her willingness to take the initiative, to strike out on her own in the face of adversity and uncertainty, makes her one of the strongest characters in the novel, despite her minor role. Like her father and the monster, Safie is an outsider; unlike them, she manages to gain acceptance. Additionally, Shelley's depiction of her character contains a strong cross-cultural value judgment. It esteems European culture, with its flexibility, openness, and opportunities for women, over Arab or Muslim culture, with its rigidity, self-enclosed quality, and strict gender prescriptions.

CHAPTERS 15–17

SUMMARY: CHAPTER 15

While foraging for food in the woods around the cottage one night, the monster finds an abandoned leather satchel containing some clothes and books. Eager to learn more about the world than he can discover through the chink in the cottage wall, he brings the books back to his hovel and begins to read. The books include Johann Wolfgang von Goethe's *Sorrows of Werter,* a volume of Plutarch's *Lives,* and John Milton's *Paradise Lost,* the last of which has the most profound effect on the monster. Unaware that *Paradise Lost* is a work of imagination, he reads it as a factual history and finds much similarity between the story and his own situation. Rifling through the pockets of his own clothes, stolen long ago from Victor's apartment, he finds some papers from Victor's journal. With his newfound ability to read, he soon understands the horrific manner of his own creation and the disgust with which his creator regarded him.

Dismayed by these discoveries, the monster wishes to reveal himself to the cottagers in the hope that they will see past his hideous exterior and befriend him. He decides to approach the blind De Lacey first, hoping to win him over while Felix, Agatha, and Safie are away. He believes that De Lacey, unprejudiced against his hideous exterior, may be able to convince the others of his gentle nature.

The perfect opportunity soon presents itself, as Felix, Agatha, and Safie depart one day for a long walk. The monster nervously enters the cottage and begins to speak to the old man. Just as he begins to explain his situation, however, the other three return unexpectedly. Felix drives the monster away, horrified by his appearance.

SUMMARY: CHAPTER 16

In the wake of this rejection, the monster swears to revenge himself against all human beings, his creator in particular. Journeying for months out of sight of others, he makes his way toward Geneva. On the way, he spots a young girl, seemingly alone; the girl slips into a stream and appears to be on the verge of drowning. When the monster rescues the girl from the water, the man accompanying her, suspecting him of having attacked her, shoots him.

As he nears Geneva, the monster runs across Victor's younger brother, William, in the woods. When William mentions that his father is Alphonse Frankenstein, the monster erupts in a rage of vengeance and strangles the boy to death with his bare hands. He takes a picture of Caroline Frankenstein that the boy has been holding and places it in the folds of the dress of a girl sleeping in a barn—Justine Moritz, who is later executed for William's murder.

Having explained to Victor the circumstances behind William's murder and Justine's conviction, the monster implores Victor to create another monster to accompany him and be his mate.

SUMMARY: CHAPTER 17

The monster tells Victor that it is his right to have a female monster companion. Victor refuses at first, but the monster appeals to Victor's sense of responsibility as his creator. He tells Victor that all of his evil actions have been the result of a desperate loneliness. He promises to take his new mate to South America to hide in the jungle far from human contact. With the sympathy of a fellow monster, he argues, he will no longer be compelled to kill. Convinced by these arguments, Victor finally agrees to create a female monster. Overjoyed but still skeptical, the monster tells Victor that he will monitor Victor's progress and that Victor need not worry about contacting him when his work is done.

ANALYSIS: CHAPTERS 15–17

Paradise Lost, here and throughout the novel, provides a touchstone for the monster as he tries to understand his identity. Comparing himself to both Adam and Satan, perceiving himself as both human and demonic, the monster is poised uncomfortably between two realms. "Like Adam," he says, "I was created apparently united by no link to any other being in existence," but "many times I considered Satan as the fitter emblem of my condition; for often, like him, when I viewed the bliss of my protectors, the bitter gall of envy rose within me." Scolded like Adam and cursed like Satan, the monster is painfully aware of his creator's utter disdain for him.

The monster continues to address Victor directly, reminding the reader of the relationship between the two, the concrete situation in which the monster's story is being told (the hut on Montanvert), and the complicated narrative structure of the novel. Furthermore, quotes like "Unfeeling, heartless creator! You had endowed me with perceptions and passions, and then cast me abroad an object for the scorn and horror of mankind" serve not only to structure the narrative formally but also to emphasize that the monster has a purpose in telling his story: he wants to elicit a reaction from Victor, a recognition of Victor's responsibility for his disastrous plight.

The theme of sublime nature reappears in the monster's narrative, and nature's ability to affect the monster powerfully, as it does Victor, humanizes him. It is worth noting that whereas Victor seeks the high, cold, hard world of the Alps for comfort, as if to freeze (and hence incapacitate) his guilt about the murder, the monster finds solace in the soft colors and smells of a springtime forest, symbolizing his desire to reveal himself to the world and interact with others. "Half surprised by the novelty of these sensations, I allowed myself to be borne away by them; and, forgetting my solitude and deformity, dared to be happy," the monster says. Unlike Victor, he is able to push away, at least temporarily, the negative aspects of his existence.

CHAPTERS 18–20

SUMMARY: CHAPTER 18

After his fateful meeting with the monster on the glacier, Victor puts off the creation of a new, female creature. He begins to have doubts about the wisdom of agreeing to the monster's request. He realizes that the project will require him to travel to England to gather information. His father notices that his spirits are troubled much of the time—Victor, still racked by guilt over the deaths of William and Justine, is now newly horrified by the task in which he is about to engage—and asks him if his impending marriage to Elizabeth is the source of his melancholy. Victor assures him that the prospect of marriage to Elizabeth is the only happiness in his life. Eager to raise Victor's spirits, Alphonse suggests that they celebrate the marriage immediately. Victor refuses, unwilling to marry Elizabeth until he has completed his obligation to the monster. He asks Alphonse if he can first travel to England, and Alphonse consents.

Victor and Alphonse arrange a two-year tour, on which Henry Clerval, eager to begin his studies after several years of unpleasant work for his father in Geneva, will accompany Victor. After traveling for a while, they reach London.

SUMMARY: CHAPTER 19

Victor and Henry journey through England and Scotland, but Victor grows impatient to begin his work and free himself of his bond to the monster. Victor has an acquaintance in a Scottish town, with whom he urges Henry to stay while he goes alone on a tour of Scotland. Henry consents reluctantly, and Victor departs for a remote, desolate island in the Orkneys to complete his project.

Quickly setting up a laboratory in a small shack, Victor devotes many hours to working on his new creature. He often has trouble continuing his work, however, knowing how unsatisfying, even grotesque, the product of his labor will be.

SUMMARY: CHAPTER 20

While working one night, Victor begins to think about what might happen after he finishes his creation. He imagines that his new creature might not want to seclude herself, as the monster had promised, or that the two creatures might have children, creating "a race of devils . . . on the earth." In the midst of these reflections and growing concern, Victor looks up to see the monster grinning at him through the window. Overcome by the monster's hideousness and the possibility of a second creature like him, he destroys his work in progress. The monster becomes enraged at Victor for breaking his promise, and at the prospect of his own continued solitude. He curses and vows revenge, then departs, swearing that he will be with Victor on his wedding night.

The following night, Victor receives a letter from Henry, who, tired of Scotland, suggests that they continue their travels. Before he leaves his shack, Victor cleans and packs his chemical instruments and collects the remains of his second creature. Late that evening, he rows out onto the ocean and throws the remains into the water, allowing himself to rest in the boat for a while. When he wakes, he finds that the winds will not permit him to return to shore. Panicking, in fear for his life, he contemplates the possibility of dying at sea, blown far out into the Atlantic. Soon the winds change, however, and he reaches shore near a town. When he lands, a group of townspeople greet him rudely, telling him that he is under suspicion for a murder discovered the previous night.

ANALYSIS: CHAPTERS 18–20

The contrast, first established at Ingolstadt, between the inwardly focused Victor and the outwardly focused Henry sharpens as the natural world produces differing effects in the two men. Earlier, Henry's interaction with the Frankenstein family and general sociability counter Victor's secrecy and self-isolation. Similarly, his optimism and cheer in the presence of sublime nature now counter the anxiety that Victor feels in knowing that the monster pervades his natural surroundings. For Henry, "alive to every new scene; joyful when he saw the beauties of the setting sun, and more happy when he beheld it rise," nature is a source of infinite bliss, while for Victor it has become an unending reminder of his imprudent meddling, and of his responsibility for the tragedies that have plagued him.

An appreciation of nature is not the only aspect of Victor's character that Henry seems to have adopted: Henry is now enthusiastic about natural philosophy and eager to explore the world—much like Victor had been two years before. Victor himself notes that "in Clerval I saw the image of my former self." One can argue that Henry represents the impending ruin of another young, brilliant man by science; one can also argue that he represents the healthy, safe route to scientific knowledge that Victor never took. In either case, Victor's emotional outbursts strongly foreshadow Henry's death: "And where does he now exist?" he asks. "Is this gentle and lovely being lost forever?"

The pervading theme of the passive, innocent woman—manifested in the mother who sacrifices herself for her daughter, the fiancée who waits endlessly for her future husband, and the orphan girl who is rescued from poverty—culminates in this section with the female monster whose creation Victor suddenly aborts after being struck by doubts about the correctness of his actions. Though never alive, the female monster is a powerful presence: to Victor, she represents another crime against humanity and nature; to the monster, she represents his one remaining hope for a life not spent alone. Even Victor, as he tears his creation apart, recognizes her near-humanity: "I almost felt," he says, "as if I had mangled the living flesh of a human being." Victor's decision to destroy the female creature can be seen as an explicitly anti-feminist action. He fears her ability to reproduce (and thereby create a "race of devils"); he fears that, as a woman, she will refuse to satisfy the male monster for whom she has been created; and he fears that he will unleash another power into the world that he cannot control. Unlike the God of Genesis, who creates a woman to keep Adam company, Victor does not have ultimate power over his creations. His anxiety leads him to project a stereotypically male activeness onto the female creature; his decision to destroy her ensures her absolute passivity.

Victor sprinkles his speech with metanarrative comments that remind the reader of the relationship between storyteller and audience, shape the upcoming narrative, and demonstrate the narrator's deep emotional investment in his story. "I must pause here; for it requires all my fortitude to recall the memory of the frightful events which I am about to relate, in proper detail, to my recollection," Victor says, illustrating that he is overwhelmed by emotion and offering a glimpse of the horrific story that he is about to tell. Victor's apostrophes to his absent friends serve the same purposes, adding to the emotional impact of his speech, emphasizing the poignancy of his nostalgic memories, and calling attention to the layered narrative. When Victor cries out "Clerval! Beloved Friend! Even now it delights me to record your words," the reader senses the power of Victor's emotion and its ultimate uselessness against the force of fate. Additionally, the mention of "record[ing]" Henry's words underscores the fact that it is only through Walton that the reader has access to the other characters and their narratives.

CHAPTERS 21–23

SUMMARY: CHAPTER 21

After confronting Victor, the townspeople take him to Mr. Kirwin, the town magistrate. Victor hears witnesses testify against him, claiming that they found the body of a man along the beach the previous night and that, just before finding the body, they saw a boat in the water that resembled Victor's. Mr. Kirwin decides to bring Victor to look at the body to see what effect it has on him: if Victor is the murderer, perhaps he will react with visible emotion. When Victor sees the body, he does indeed react with horror, for the victim is Henry Clerval, with the black marks of the monster's hands around his neck. In shock, Victor falls into convulsions and suffers a long illness.

Victor remains ill for two months. Upon his recovery, he finds himself still in prison. Mr. Kirwin, now compassionate and much more sympathetic than before Victor's illness, visits him in his cell. He tells him that he has a visitor, and for a moment Victor fears that the monster has come to cause him even more misery. The visitor turns out to be his father, who, upon hearing of his son's illness and the death of his friend, rushed from Geneva to see him.

Victor is overjoyed to see his father, who stays with him until the court, having nothing but circumstantial evidence, finds him innocent of Henry's murder. After his release, Victor departs with his father for Geneva.

SUMMARY: CHAPTER 22

On their way home, father and son stop in Paris, where Victor rests to recover his strength. Just before leaving again for Geneva, Victor receives a letter from Elizabeth. Worried by Victor's recurrent illnesses, she asks him if he is in love with another, to which Victor replies that she is the source of his joy. The letter reminds him of the monster's threat that he will be with Victor on his wedding night. He believes that the monster intends to attack him and resolves that he will fight back. Whichever one of them is destroyed, his misery will at last come to an end.

Eventually, Victor and his father arrive home and begin planning the wedding. Elizabeth is still worried about Victor, but he assures her that all will be well after the wedding. He has a terrible secret, he tells her, that he can only reveal to her after they are married. As the wedding day approaches, Victor grows more and more nervous about his impending confrontation with the monster. Finally, the wedding takes place, and Victor and Elizabeth depart for a family cottage to spend the night.

SUMMARY: CHAPTER 23

In the evening, Victor and Elizabeth walk around the grounds, but Victor can think of nothing but the monster's imminent arrival. Inside, Victor worries that Elizabeth might be upset by the monster's appearance and the battle between them. He tells her to retire for the night. He begins to search for the monster in the house, when suddenly he hears Elizabeth scream and realizes that it was never his death that the monster had been intending this night. Consumed with grief over Elizabeth's death, Victor returns home and tells his father the gruesome news. Shocked by the tragic end of what should have been a joyous day, his father dies a few days later. Victor finally breaks his secrecy and tries to convince a magistrate in Geneva that an unnatural monster is responsible for the death of Elizabeth, but the magistrate does not believe him. Victor resolves to devote the rest of his life to finding and destroying the monster.

ANALYSIS: CHAPTERS 21–23

Victor's pattern of falling into extended illness in reaction to the monster suggests that the deterioration of his health is, to some extent, psychologically induced—as if guilt prevents him from facing fully the horribleness of the monster and his deeds. "The human frame could no longer support the agonizing suffering that I endured, and I was carried out of the room in strong convulsions," he recounts of his despair at seeing Henry's corpse, making an explicit link between psychological torment and physical infirmity. That Victor also falls ill soon after creating the monster and experiences a decline in health after the deaths of William and Justine points toward guilt as the trigger for this psychological mechanism.

Henry again serves as a link between Victor and society, as his death brings Alphonse to visit his son. "Nothing, at this moment, could have given me greater pleasure than the arrival of my father," Victor says. As a result of spending so much time in Ingolstadt ignoring his family, and also as a result of the monster's depredations, Victor becomes aware of the importance of interaction with family and friends. Having failed to inspire love in Victor, the monster seeks to establish a relationship with his creator that would force his creator to feel his pain. By destroying those people dear to Victor, the monster, acutely aware of the meaningfulness of social interaction, brings Victor closer and closer to the state of solitude that he himself has experienced since being created.

Victor's formerly intense connection with sublime nature continues to fade, providing him no refuge from the horror of the monster's deeds. No longer an enlightening or elevating source of inspiration or consolation, the natural world becomes a mere landscape within which Victor's tragic dance with the monster plays itself out. The barren Arctic wasteland into which Victor soon chases the monster embodies the raw and primal quality of his hatred for his creation and becomes the final, inescapable resting place for both man and monster.

The murder of Elizabeth forms the climax of the novel, as it is the moment in which the monster finally succeeds in obliterating Victor's social world. With his family, best friend, and faith in science snatched away from him, Victor can derive meaning in life only from his hatred of the monster. The crucial transition has been made: stripped of Elizabeth, the last, and most important, element of his life, Victor becomes dehumanized and develops an obsessive thirst for revenge similar to that exhibited previously by the monster.

CHAPTER 24 & WALTON, IN CONTINUATION

SUMMARY: CHAPTER 24

His whole family destroyed, Victor decides to leave Geneva and the painful memories it holds behind him forever. He tracks the monster for months, guided by slight clues, messages, and hints that the monster leaves for him. Angered by these taunts, Victor continues his pursuit into the ice and snow of the North. There he meets Walton and tells his story. He entreats Walton to continue his search for vengeance after he is dead.

SUMMARY: WALTON, IN CONTINUATION

> *I, the miserable and the abandoned, am an abortion, to be spurned at, and kicked, and trampled on.*
>
> *(See* QUOTATIONS, *p. 46)*

Walton then regains control of the narrative, continuing the story in the form of further letters to his sister. He tells her that he believes in the truth of Victor's story. He laments that he did not know Victor, who remains on the brink of death, in better days.

One morning, Walton's crewmen enter his cabin and beg him to promise that they will return to England if they break out of the ice in which they have been trapped ever since the night they first saw the monster's sledge. Victor speaks up, however, and convinces the men that the glory and honor of their quest should be enough motivation for them to continue toward their goal. They are momentarily moved, but two days later they again entreat Walton, who consents to the plan of return.

Just before the ship is set to head back to England, Victor dies. Several days later, Walton hears a strange sound coming from the room in which Victor's body lies. Investigating the noise, Walton is startled to find the monster, as hideous as Victor had described, weeping over his dead creator's body. The monster begins to tell him of all his sufferings. He says that he deeply regrets having become an instrument of evil and that, with his creator dead, he is ready to die. He leaves the ship and departs into the darkness.

ANALYSIS: CHAPTER 24 & WALTON, IN CONTINUATION

By this point in the novel, Victor has assumed the very inhumanity of which he accuses the monster. Just as the monster earlier haunts

Victor, seeking revenge on him for having destroyed any possibility of a mate for him, Victor now experiences an obsessive need to exact revenge on the monster for murdering his loved ones. Like the monster, he finds himself utterly alone in the world, with nothing but hatred of his nemesis to sustain him.

Echoes of the monster's earlier statements now appear in Victor's speech, illustrating the extent to which Victor has become dehumanized. "I was cursed by some devil," he cries, "and carried about with me my eternal hell." This is the second allusion to the passage in Paradise Lost in which Satan, cast out from Heaven, says that he himself is Hell. The first allusion, made by the monster after being repulsed by the cottagers, is nearly identical: "I, like the arch fiend, bore a hell within me." Driven by their hatred, the two monsters—Victor and his creation—move farther and farther away from human society and sanity.

The final section of the novel, in which Walton continues the story, completes the framing narrative. Walton's perception of Victor as a great, noble man ruined by the events described in the story adds to the tragic conclusion of the novel. The technique of framing narratives within narratives not only allows the reader to hear the voices of all of the main characters, but also provides multiple views of the central characters. Walton sees Frankenstein as a noble, tragic figure; Frankenstein sees himself as an overly proud and overly ambitious victim of fate; the monster sees Frankenstein as a reckless creator, too self-centered to care for his creation.

Similarly, while Walton and Frankenstein deem the monster a malevolent, insensitive brute, the monster casts himself as a martyred classical hero: "I shall ascend my funeral pile triumphantly and exult in the agony of the torturing flames," he says. Fittingly, the last few pages of the novel are taken up with the monster's own words as he attempts to gain self-definition before leaving for the northern ice to die. That the monster reassumes control of the narrative from Walton ensures that, after Victor's death and even after his own, the struggle to understand who or what the monster really is—Adam or Satan, tragic victim or arch-villain—will go on.

IMPORTANT QUOTATIONS EXPLAINED

1. I saw—with shut eyes, but acute mental vision—I saw the pale student of unhallowed arts kneeling beside the thing he had put together. I saw the hideous phantasm of a man stretched out, and then, on the working of some powerful engine, show signs of life and stir with an uneasy, half-vital motion. Frightful must it be, for supremely frightful would be the effect of any human endeavor to mock the stupendous mechanism of the Creator of the world.

Taken from Mary Shelley's Author's Introduction to the 1831 edition of *Frankenstein,* this quote describes the vision that inspired the novel and the prototypes for Victor and the monster. Shelley's image evokes some of the key themes, such as the utter unnaturalness of the monster ("an uneasy, half-vital motion"), the relationship between creator and created ("kneeling beside the thing he had put together"), and the dangerous consequences of misused knowledge ("supremely frightful would be the effect of . . . mock[ing] . . . the Creator").

2. Did I request thee, Maker, from my clay
    To mould me Man, did I solicit thee
    From darkness to promote me?

These lines appear on the title page of the novel and come from John Milton's *Paradise Lost,* when Adam bemoans his fallen condition (Book X, 743–745). The monster conceives of himself as a tragic figure, comparing himself to both Adam and Satan. Like Adam, he is shunned by his creator, though he strives to be good. These rhetorical questions epitomize the monster's ill will toward Victor for abandoning him in a world relentlessly hostile to him and foist responsibility for his ugliness and eventual evil upon Victor.

3.   What may not be expected in a country of eternal light?

This quote comes from Walton's first letter to his sister in England. It encapsulates one of the main themes of *Frankenstein*—that of light as a symbol of knowledge and discovery. Walton's quest to reach the northernmost part of the earth is similar in spirit to Victor's quest for the secret of life: both seek ultimate knowledge, and both sacrifice the comfort of the realm of known knowledge in their respective pursuits. Additionally, the beauty and simplicity of the phrasing epitomize the eighteenth-century scientific rationalists' optimism about, and trust in, knowledge as a pure good.

4.   So much has been done, exclaimed the soul of
      Frankenstein—more, far more, will I achieve; treading in
      the steps already marked, I will pioneer a new way, explore
      unknown powers, and unfold to the world the deepest
      mysteries of creation.

Victor utters these words in Chapter 3 as he relates to Walton how his chemistry professor, M. Waldman, ignited in him an irrepressible desire to gain knowledge of the secret of life. Victor's reference to himself in the third person illustrates his sense of fatalism—he is driven by his passion, unable to control it. Further, the glorious, assertive quality of his statement foreshadows the fact that Victor's passion will not be tempered by any consideration of the possible horrific consequences of his search for knowledge. Additionally, this declaration furthers the parallel between Walton's spatial explorations and Frankenstein's forays into unknown knowledge, as both men seek to "pioneer a new way," to make progress beyond established limits.

5.   I, the miserable and the abandoned, am an abortion, to be
      spurned at, and kicked, and trampled on.

In Walton's final letter to his sister, he recounts the words that the monster speaks to him over Victor's dead body. This eruption of angry self-pity as the monster questions the injustice of how he has been treated compellingly captures his inner life, giving Walton and the reader a glimpse into the suffering that has motivated his crimes. This line also evokes the motif of abortion: the monster is an unwanted life, a creation abandoned and shunned by his creator.

QUOTATIONS

KEY FACTS

FULL TITLE
Frankenstein: or, The Modern Prometheus

AUTHOR
Mary Wollstonecraft Shelley

TYPE OF WORK
Novel

GENRE
Gothic science fiction

LANGUAGE
English

TIME AND PLACE WRITTEN
Switzerland, 1816, and London, 1816–1817

DATE OF FIRST PUBLICATION
January 1, 1818

PUBLISHER
Lackington, Hughes, Harding, Mavor, & Jones

NARRATOR
The primary narrator is Robert Walton, who, in his letters, quotes Victor Frankenstein's first-person narrative at length; Victor, in turn, quotes the monster's first-person narrative; in addition, the lesser characters Elizabeth Lavenza and Alphonse Frankenstein narrate parts of the story through their letters to Victor.

CLIMAX
The murder of Elizabeth Lavenza on the night of her wedding to Victor Frankenstein in Chapter 23

PROTAGONIST
Victor Frankenstein

ANTAGONIST
Frankenstein's monster

KEY FACTS

SETTING (TIME)
Eighteenth century

SETTING (PLACE)
Geneva; the Swiss Alps; Ingolstadt; England and Scotland; the northern ice

POINT OF VIEW
The point of view shifts with the narration, from Robert Walton to Victor Frankenstein to Frankenstein's monster, then back to Walton, with a few digressions in the form of letters from Elizabeth Lavenza and Alphonse Frankenstein.

FALLING ACTION
After the murder of Elizabeth Lavenza, when Victor Frankenstein chases the monster to the northern ice, is rescued by Robert Walton, narrates his story, and dies

TENSE
Past

FORESHADOWING
Ubiquitous—throughout his narrative, Victor uses words such as "fate" and "omen" to hint at the tragedy that has befallen him; additionally, he occasionally pauses in his recounting to collect himself in the face of frightening memories.

TONE
Gothic, Romantic, emotional, tragic, fatalistic

THEMES
Dangerous knowledge; sublime nature; texts; secrecy; monstrosity

MOTIFS
Passive women; abortion

SYMBOLS
Fire and light

Study Questions

1. *Discuss the novel's shifts in narrative perspective. What is the effect of presenting different characters' viewpoints, especially those of Victor and the monster?*

Narrative in *Frankenstein* shifts from Robert Walton to Victor Frankenstein to the monster and finally back to Walton. With each shift of perspective, the reader gains new information about both the facts of the story and the personalities of the respective narrators. Each narrator adds pieces of information that only he knows: Walton explains the circumstances of Victor's last days; Victor explains his creation of the monster; the monster explains his turn to evil. The differences in perspective between the narrators are sometimes stark, especially since Victor and the monster stand in opposition to each other for much of the novel.

From Victor's point of view, the monster is nothing but a hideous and evil creature; from the monster's account, on the other hand, it becomes clear that he is a thinking, feeling, emotional being. The recounting of the murder of William Frankenstein is a prime example of the impact of perspective: while Victor's description, colored by the emotional letter from his father, focuses on the absolute evil of the act, the monster's version of events centers on the emotional circumstances surrounding it. Even if one cannot sympathize with the monster, one can at least understand his actions. This kind of dual narration is one of the more interesting consequences of the complicated narrative structure that Shelley implements.

2. *Trace and discuss the role of letters and written communication throughout the novel.*

The entirety of *Frankenstein* is contained within Robert Walton's letters, which record the narratives of both Frankenstein and the monster, to his sister (even Shelley's preface to the book can be read as an introductory letter). Walton's epistolary efforts frame Victor's narrative, which includes letters from Alphonse and Elizabeth. Like Walton's, these letters convey important information that serves to advance the plot and offer some sense of authenticity to an implausible story. Additionally, Victor's inclusion of these personal letters in his narrative allows Alphonse and Elizabeth to express themselves, shedding light on their respective concerns and attitudes, and thus rendering them more human.

Shelley's use of letters enables the shift of narrative from one character to another while remaining within the bounds of the standard novel. Letters also serve as a means of social interaction, as characters are frequently out of immediate contact with one another. Walton never encounters his sister in the novel; his relationship with her is based wholly on correspondence. Likewise, Victor often isolates himself from his loved ones; the letters from Alphonse and Elizabeth mark attempts to connect with him. Even the monster uses written communication to develop a relationship with Victor when, at the end of the novel, he leads him ever northward by means of notes on the trees and rocks he passes.

3.   *Discuss the presentation of women in the novel. Do Victor and the monster differ in their view of women, and if so, how?*

Women in *Frankenstein* are generally pure, innocent, and passive. Though there are a few exceptions, such as Caroline Beaufort, who works to support her impoverished father, women are generally seen as kind but powerless. For example, Elizabeth stands up for Justine's innocence but cannot prevent her execution. For both Victor and the monster, woman is the ultimate companion, providing comfort and acceptance. For Victor, Elizabeth proves the sole joy that can alleviate his guilty conscience; similarly, the monster seeks a female of his kind to commiserate with his awful existence. Each eventually destroys the other's love interest, transferring woman's status from object of desire to object of revenge; women thus are never given the opportunity to act on their own.

In the context of passive female characters, it is interesting to note that Mary Shelley's mother, Mary Wollstonecraft, was the author of the strongly feminist *A Vindication of the Rights of Woman*. One can argue that Frankenstein represents a rejection of the male attempt to usurp (by unnatural means) what is properly a female endeavor—birth. One can also interpret the novel as a broader rejection of the aggressive, rational, and male-dominated science of the late seventeenth and early eighteenth century. Though it was long met with mistrust, this science increasingly shaped European society. In this light, *Frankenstein* can be seen as prioritizing traditional female domesticity with its emphasis on family and interpersonal relationships.

How to Write Literary Analysis

The Literary Essay: A Step-by-Step Guide

When you read for pleasure, your only goal is enjoyment. You might find yourself reading to get caught up in an exciting story, to learn about an interesting time or place, or just to pass time. Maybe you're looking for inspiration, guidance, or a reflection of your own life. There are as many different, valid ways of reading a book as there are books in the world.

When you read a work of literature in an English class, however, you're being asked to read in a special way: you're being asked to perform *literary analysis*. To analyze something means to break it down into smaller parts and then examine how those parts work, both individually and together. Literary analysis involves examining all the parts of a novel, play, short story, or poem—elements such as character, setting, tone, and imagery—and thinking about how the author uses those elements to create certain effects.

A literary essay isn't a book review: you're not being asked whether or not you liked a book or whether you'd recommend it to another reader. A literary essay also isn't like the kind of book report you wrote when you were younger, where your teacher wanted you to summarize the book's action. A high school- or college-level literary essay asks, "How does this piece of literature actually work?" "How does it do what it does?" and, "Why might the author have made the choices he or she did?"

The Seven Steps

No one is born knowing how to analyze literature; it's a skill you learn and a process you can master. As you gain more practice with this kind of thinking and writing, you'll be able to craft a method that works best for you. But until then, here are seven basic steps to writing a well-constructed literary essay:

1. Ask questions
2. Collect evidence
3. Construct a thesis

53

4. Develop and organize arguments
5. Write the introduction
6. Write the body paragraphs
7. Write the conclusion

──────────────

1. Ask Questions

When you're assigned a literary essay in class, your teacher will often provide you with a list of writing prompts. Lucky you! Now all you have to do is choose one. Do yourself a favor and pick a topic that interests you. You'll have a much better (not to mention easier) time if you start off with something you enjoy thinking about. If you are asked to come up with a topic by yourself, though, you might start to feel a little panicked. Maybe you have too many ideas—or none at all. Don't worry. Take a deep breath and start by asking yourself these questions:

- **What struck you?** Did a particular image, line, or scene linger in your mind for a long time? If it fascinated you, chances are you can draw on it to write a fascinating essay.

- **What confused you?** Maybe you were surprised to see a character act in a certain way, or maybe you didn't understand why the book ended the way it did. Confusing moments in a work of literature are like a loose thread in a sweater: if you pull on it, you can unravel the entire thing. Ask yourself why the author chose to write about that character or scene the way he or she did and you might tap into some important insights about the work as a whole.

- **Did you notice any patterns?** Is there a phrase that the main character uses constantly or an image that repeats throughout the book? If you can figure out how that pattern weaves through the work and what the significance of that pattern is, you've almost got your entire essay mapped out.

- **Did you notice any contradictions or ironies?** Great works of literature are complex; great literary essays recognize and explain those complexities. Maybe the title (*Happy Days*) totally disagrees with the book's subject matter (hungry orphans dying in the woods). Maybe the main character acts one way around his family and a completely different way around his friends and associates. If you can find a way to explain a work's contradictory elements, you've got the seeds of a great essay.

At this point, you don't need to know exactly what you're going to say about your topic; you just need a place to begin your exploration. You can help direct your reading and brainstorming by formulating your topic as a *question,* which you'll then try to answer in your essay. The best questions invite critical debates and discussions, not just a rehashing of the summary. Remember, you're looking for something you can *prove or argue* based on evidence you find in the text. Finally, remember to keep the scope of your question in mind: is this a topic you can adequately address within the word or page limit you've been given? Conversely, is this a topic big enough to fill the required length?

GOOD QUESTIONS

"Are Romeo and Juliet's parents responsible for the deaths of their children?"

"Why do pigs keep showing up in LORD OF THE FLIES?*"*

"Are Dr. Frankenstein and his monster alike? How?"

BAD QUESTIONS

"What happens to Scout in TO KILL A MOCKINGBIRD?*"*

"What do the other characters in JULIUS CAESAR *think about Caesar?"*

"How does Hester Prynne in THE SCARLET LETTER *remind me of my sister?"*

---

2. COLLECT EVIDENCE

Once you know what question you want to answer, it's time to scour the book for things that will help you answer the question. Don't worry if you don't know what you want to say yet—right now you're just collecting ideas and material and letting it all percolate. Keep track of passages, symbols, images, or scenes that deal with your topic. Eventually, you'll start making connections between these examples and your thesis will emerge.

Here's a brief summary of the various parts that compose each and every work of literature. These are the elements that you will analyze in your essay, and which you will offer as evidence to support your arguments. For more on the parts of literary works, see the Glossary of Literary Terms at the end of this section.

ELEMENTS OF STORY These are the *what*s of the work—what happens, where it happens, and to whom it happens.

- **Plot:** All of the events and actions of the work.
- **Character:** The people who act and are acted upon in a literary work. The main character of a work is known as the *protagonist*.
- **Conflict:** The central tension in the work. In most cases, the protagonist wants something, while opposing forces (antagonists) hinder the protagonist's progress.
- **Setting:** When and where the work takes place. Elements of setting include location, time period, time of day, weather, social atmosphere, and economic conditions.
- **Narrator:** The person telling the story. The narrator may straightforwardly report what happens, convey the subjective opinions and perceptions of one or more characters, or provide commentary and opinion in his or her own voice.
- **Themes:** The main idea or message of the work—usually an abstract idea about people, society, or life in general. A work may have many themes, which may be in tension with one another.

ELEMENTS OF STYLE These are the *how*s—how the characters speak, how the story is constructed, and how language is used throughout the work.

- **Structure and organization:** How the parts of the work are assembled. Some novels are narrated in a linear, chronological fashion, while others skip around in time. Some plays follow a traditional three- or five-act structure, while others are a series of loosely connected scenes. Some authors deliberately leave gaps in their works, leaving readers to puzzle out the missing information. A work's structure and organization can tell you a lot about the kind of message it wants to convey.
- **Point of view:** The perspective from which a story is told. In *first-person point of view*, the narrator involves him or herself in the story. ("I went to the store"; "We watched in horror as the bird slammed into the window.") A first-person narrator is usually the protagonist of the work, but not always. In *third-person point of view*, the narrator does not participate

in the story. A third-person narrator may closely follow a specific character, recounting that individual character's thoughts or experiences, or it may be what we call an *omniscient* narrator. Omniscient narrators see and know all: they can witness any event in any time or place and are privy to the inner thoughts and feelings of all characters. Remember that the narrator and the author are not the same thing!

- **Diction:** Word choice. Whether a character uses dry, clinical language or flowery prose with lots of exclamation points can tell you a lot about his or her attitude and personality.

- **Syntax:** Word order and sentence construction. Syntax is a crucial part of establishing an author's narrative voice. Ernest Hemingway, for example, is known for writing in very short, straightforward sentences, while James Joyce characteristically wrote in long, incredibly complicated lines.

- **Tone:** The mood or feeling of the text. Diction and syntax often contribute to the tone of a work. A novel written in short, clipped sentences that use small, simple words might feel brusque, cold, or matter-of-fact.

- **Imagery:** Language that appeals to the senses, representing things that can be seen, smelled, heard, tasted, or touched.

- **Figurative language:** Language that is not meant to be interpreted literally. The most common types of figurative language are *metaphors* and *similes,* which compare two unlike things in order to suggest a similarity between them—for example, "All the world's a stage," or "The moon is like a ball of green cheese." (Metaphors say one thing *is* another thing; similes claim that one thing is *like* another thing.)

---

3. CONSTRUCT A THESIS

When you've examined all the evidence you've collected and know how you want to answer the question, it's time to write your thesis statement. A *thesis* is a claim about a work of literature that needs to be supported by evidence and arguments. The thesis statement is the heart of the literary essay, and the bulk of your paper will be spent trying to prove this claim. A good thesis will be:

- **Arguable.** "*The Great Gatsby* describes New York society in the 1920s" isn't a thesis—it's a fact.

- **Provable through textual evidence**. "*Hamlet* is a confusing but ultimately very well-written play" is a weak thesis because it offers the writer's personal opinion about the book. Yes, it's arguable, but it's not a claim that can be proved or supported with examples taken from the play itself.

- **Surprising**. "Both George and Lenny change a great deal in *Of Mice and Men*" is a weak thesis because it's obvious. A really strong thesis will argue for a reading of the text that is not immediately apparent.

- **Specific**. "Dr. Frankenstein's monster tells us a lot about the human condition" is *almost* a really great thesis statement, but it's still too vague. What does the writer mean by "a lot"? *How* does the monster tell us so much about the human condition?

GOOD THESIS STATEMENTS

Question: In *Romeo and Juliet*, which is more powerful in shaping the lovers' story: fate or foolishness?

Thesis: "Though Shakespeare defines Romeo and Juliet as 'star-crossed lovers' and images of stars and planets appear throughout the play, a closer examination of that celestial imagery reveals that the stars are merely witnesses to the characters' foolish activities and not the causes themselves."

Question: How does the bell jar function as a symbol in Sylvia Plath's *The Bell Jar*?

Thesis: "A bell jar is a bell-shaped glass that has three basic uses: to hold a specimen for observation, to contain gases, and to maintain a vacuum. The bell jar appears in each of these capacities in *The Bell Jar*, Plath's semi-autobiographical novel, and each appearance marks a different stage in Esther's mental breakdown."

Question: Would Piggy in *The Lord of the Flies* make a good island leader if he were given the chance?

Thesis: "Though the intelligent, rational, and innovative Piggy has the mental characteristics of a good leader, he ultimately lacks the social skills necessary to be an effective one. Golding emphasizes this point by giving Piggy a foil in the charismatic Jack, whose magnetic personality allows him to capture and wield power effectively, if not always wisely."

4. DEVELOP AND ORGANIZE ARGUMENTS

The reasons and examples that support your thesis will form the middle paragraphs of your essay. Since you can't really write your thesis statement until you know how you'll structure your argument, you'll probably end up working on steps 3 and 4 at the same time.

There's no single method of argumentation that will work in every context. One essay prompt might ask you to compare and contrast two characters, while another asks you to trace an image through a given work of literature. These questions require different kinds of answers and therefore different kinds of arguments. Below, we'll discuss three common kinds of essay prompts and some strategies for constructing a solid, well-argued case.

TYPES OF LITERARY ESSAYS

- **Compare and contrast**

  Compare and contrast the characters of Huck and Jim in THE ADVENTURES OF HUCKLEBERRY FINN.

  Chances are you've written this kind of essay before. In an academic literary context, you'll organize your arguments the same way you would in any other class. You can either go *subject by subject* or *point by point*. In the former, you'll discuss one character first and then the second. In the latter, you'll choose several traits (attitude toward life, social status, images and metaphors associated with the character) and devote a paragraph to each. You may want to use a mix of these two approaches—for example, you may want to spend a paragraph a piece broadly sketching Huck's and Jim's personalities before transitioning into a paragraph or two that describes a few key points of comparison. This can be a highly effective strategy if you want to make a counterintuitive argument—that, despite seeming to be totally different, the two objects being compared are actually similar in a very important way (or vice versa). Remember that your essay should reveal something fresh or unexpected about the text, so think beyond the obvious parallels and differences.

- **Trace**

  Choose an image—for example, birds, knives, or eyes—and trace that image throughout MACBETH.

  Sounds pretty easy, right? All you need to do is read the play, underline every appearance of a knife in *Macbeth,* and then list them in your essay in the order they appear, right? Well, not exactly. Your teacher doesn't want a simple catalog of examples. He or she wants to see you make *connections* between those examples—that's the difference between summarizing and analyzing. In the *Macbeth* example above, think about the different contexts in which knives appear in the play and to what effect. In *Macbeth,* there are real knives and imagined knives; knives that kill and knives that simply threaten. Categorize and classify your examples to give them some order. Finally, always keep the overall effect in mind. After you choose and analyze your examples, you should come to some greater understanding about the work, as well as your chosen image, symbol, or phrase's role in developing the major themes and stylistic strategies of that work.

- **Debate**

  Is the society depicted in 1984 *good for its citizens?*

  In this kind of essay, you're being asked to debate a moral, ethical, or aesthetic issue regarding the work. You might be asked to judge a character or group of characters (*Is Caesar responsible for his own demise?*) or the work itself (*Is* JANE EYRE *a feminist novel?*). For this kind of essay, there are two important points to keep in mind. First, don't simply base your arguments on your personal feelings and reactions. Every literary essay expects you to read and analyze the work, so search for evidence in the text. What do characters in *1984* have to say about the government of Oceania? What images does Orwell use that might give you a hint about his attitude toward the government? As in any debate, you also need to make sure that you define all the necessary terms before you begin to argue your case. What does it mean to be a "good" society? What makes a novel "feminist"? You should define your terms right up front, in the first paragraph after your introduction.

  Second, remember that strong literary essays make contrary and surprising arguments. Try to think outside the box. In the *1984* example above, it seems like the obvious answer would be no, the totalitarian society depicted in Orwell's novel is *not* good for its citizens. But can you think of any arguments for the opposite side? Even if your final assertion is that the novel depicts a cruel, repressive, and therefore harmful society, acknowledging and responding to the counterargument will strengthen your overall case.

5. WRITE THE INTRODUCTION

Your introduction sets up the entire essay. It's where you present your topic and articulate the particular issues and questions you'll be addressing. It's also where you, as the writer, introduce yourself to your readers. A persuasive literary essay immediately establishes its writer as a knowledgeable, authoritative figure.

An introduction can vary in length depending on the overall length of the essay, but in a traditional five-paragraph essay it should be no longer than one paragraph. However long it is, your introduction needs to:

- **Provide any necessary context.** Your introduction should situate the reader and let him or her know what to expect. What book are you discussing? Which characters? What topic will you be addressing?

- **Answer the "So what?" question.** Why is this topic important, and why is your particular position on the topic noteworthy? Ideally, your introduction should pique the reader's interest by suggesting how your argument is surprising or otherwise counterintuitive. Literary essays make unexpected connections and reveal less-than-obvious truths.

- **Present your thesis.** This usually happens at or very near the end of your introduction.

- **Indicate the shape of the essay to come.** Your reader should finish reading your introduction with a good sense of the scope of your essay as well as the path you'll take toward proving your thesis. You don't need to spell out every step, but you do need to suggest the organizational pattern you'll be using.

Your introduction should not:

- **Be vague.** Beware of the two killer words in literary analysis: *interesting* and *important*. Of course the work, question, or example is interesting and important—that's why you're writing about it!

- **Open with any grandiose assertions.** Many student readers think that beginning their essays with a flamboyant statement such as, "Since the dawn of time, writers have been fascinated with the topic of free will," makes them sound important and commanding. You know what? It actually sounds pretty amateurish.

- **Wildly praise the work.** Another typical mistake student writers make is extolling the work or author. Your teacher doesn't need to be told that "Shakespeare is perhaps the greatest writer in the English language." You can mention a work's reputation in passing—by referring to *The Adventures of Huckleberry Finn* as "Mark Twain's enduring classic," for example—but don't make a point of bringing it up unless that reputation is key to your argument.

- **Go off-topic.** Keep your introduction streamlined and to the point. Don't feel the need to throw in all kinds of bells and whistles in order to impress your reader—just get to the point as quickly as you can, without skimping on any of the required steps.

---

6. WRITE THE BODY PARAGRAPHS

Once you've written your introduction, you'll take the arguments you developed in step 4 and turn them into your body paragraphs. The organization of this middle section of your essay will largely be determined by the argumentative strategy you use, but no matter how you arrange your thoughts, your body paragraphs need to do the following:

- **Begin with a strong topic sentence.** Topic sentences are like signs on a highway: they tell the reader where they are and where they're going. A good topic sentence not only alerts readers to what issue will be discussed in the following paragraph but also gives them a sense of what argument will be made *about* that issue. "Rumor and gossip play an important role in *The Crucible*" isn't a strong topic sentence because it doesn't tell us very much. "The community's constant gossiping creates an environment that allows false accusations to flourish" is a much stronger topic sentence— it not only tells us *what* the paragraph will discuss (gossip) but *how* the paragraph will discuss the topic (by showing how gossip creates a set of conditions that leads to the play's climactic action).

- **Fully and completely develop a single thought.** Don't skip around in your paragraph or try to stuff in too much material. Body paragraphs are like bricks: each individual one needs to be strong and sturdy or the entire structure will collapse. Make sure you have really proven your point before moving on to the next one.

- **Use transitions effectively.** Good literary essay writers know that each paragraph must be clearly and strongly linked to the material around it. Think of each paragraph as a response to the one that precedes it. Use transition words and phrases such as *however, similarly, on the contrary, therefore,* and *furthermore* to indicate what kind of response you're making.

---

7. WRITE THE CONCLUSION

Just as you used the introduction to ground your readers in the topic before providing your thesis, you'll use the conclusion to quickly summarize the specifics learned thus far and then hint at the broader implications of your topic. A good conclusion will:

- **Do more than simply restate the thesis.** If your thesis argued that *The Catcher in the Rye* can be read as a Christian allegory, don't simply end your essay by saying, "And that is why *The Catcher in the Rye* can be read as a Christian allegory." If you've constructed your arguments well, this kind of statement will just be redundant.

- **Synthesize the arguments, not summarize them.** Similarly, don't repeat the details of your body paragraphs in your conclusion. The reader has already read your essay, and chances are it's not so long that they've forgotten all your points by now.

- **Revisit the "So what?" question.** In your introduction, you made a case for why your topic and position are important. You should close your essay with the same sort of gesture. What do your readers know now that they didn't know before? How will that knowledge help them better appreciate or understand the work overall?

- **Move from the specific to the general.** Your essay has most likely treated a very specific element of the work—a single character, a small set of images, or a particular passage. In your conclusion, try to show how this narrow discussion has wider implications for the work overall. If your essay on *To Kill a Mockingbird* focused on the character of Boo Radley, for example, you might want to include a bit in your conclusion about how he fits into the novel's larger message about childhood, innocence, or family life.

- **Stay relevant.** Your conclusion should suggest new directions of thought, but it shouldn't be treated as an opportunity to pad your essay with all the extra, interesting ideas you came up with during your brainstorming sessions but couldn't fit into the essay proper. Don't attempt to stuff in unrelated queries or too many abstract thoughts.

- **Avoid making overblown closing statements.** A conclusion should open up your highly specific, focused discussion, but it should do so without drawing a sweeping lesson about life or human nature. Making such observations may be part of the point of reading, but it's almost always a mistake in essays, where these observations tend to sound overly dramatic or simply silly.

A+ Essay Checklist

Congratulations! If you've followed all the steps we've outlined above, you should have a solid literary essay to show for all your efforts. What if you've got your sights set on an A+? To write the kind of superlative essay that will be rewarded with a perfect grade, keep the following rubric in mind. These are the qualities that teachers expect to see in a truly A+ essay. How does yours stack up?

- ✓ Demonstrates a thorough understanding of the book
- ✓ Presents an original, compelling argument
- ✓ Thoughtfully analyzes the text's formal elements
- ✓ Uses appropriate and insightful examples
- ✓ Structures ideas in a logical and progressive order
- ✓ Demonstrates a mastery of sentence construction, transitions, grammar, spelling, and word choice

SUGGESTED ESSAY TOPICS

1. *Discuss the role of sickness in the novel. Victor often seems to fall ill after traumatic events. Is this a means of escape, and, if so, is it effective? Is there another explanation for his recurring illness?*

2. *Trace the similarities between Victor and the monster. Consider their respective relationships with nature, desires for family, and any other important parallels you find. Do Victor and the monster become more similar as the novel goes on? How does their relationship with each other develop?*

3. *Victor attributes his tragic fate to his relentless search for knowledge. Do you think that this is the true cause of his suffering? In what ways does the novel present knowledge as dangerous and destructive?*

4. *Examine the role of suspense and foreshadowing throughout the novel. Do you think these devices are effective, or does Victor's blatant foreshadowing reveal too much? How does foreshadowing differ among the three main narrators (Walton, Victor, and the monster)?*

A+ STUDENT ESSAY

> Shelley makes the monster eloquent, rather than mute or
> uncommunicative. What effect does this choice have on
> our perception of him?

The monster in Mary Shelly's *Frankenstein* lurches into life as big as a man but as ignorant as a newborn. He can't read, speak, or understand the rudiments of human interaction. When he stumbles upon the cottagers, however, he picks up language by observing them and studying their speech. It is this acquisition of language, along with the eloquence it brings, that turns the monster from a mysterious nightmare into a sympathetic and tragic figure. By showing how language transforms the monster, and by contrasting the well-spoken monster with his equally articulate creator, Shelley argues that verbal communication—rather than action or appearance—is the only way through which people can truly understand one another.

Before the monster learns to express himself, his actions are no less than terrifying. His escape from Victor's workshop seems sinister and his murder of William apparently confirms the notion that he is a powerful, malignant beast capable of unmotivated violence. His shocking appearance does not help matters. Victor assumes, and Shelley invites us to assume along with him, that this being, with his patched-together body, his yellow skin, and his black lips, must have a soul that matches his hideous appearance.

When the monster speaks, however, he throws his actions into a different light. He explains that Victor's desertion left him alone and frightened. He conveys how hurt he was when he realized that his appearance scares normal people. His stories about sympathizing with and secretly helping the cottagers show that he has an empathetic nature, and his tale of rescuing a young girl and getting a bullet for his trouble demonstrates his instinct to help those weaker than himself, sparking our outrage at society's unwarranted cruelty toward him. Even the monster's description of William's murder makes the convincing case that fury at Victor drove the monster to violence—not an excuse, by any means, but certainly an explanation that is understandable and psychologically credible. By giving the monster the power of oratory, Shelley forces us to consider his behavior from an entirely different angle and to sympathize with his plight.

LITERARY ANALYSIS

Shelley bolsters our sympathy for the monster by comparing his words to Victor's. Frankenstein is Victor's story; he has countless opportunities to argue his case and cast himself as the tragic hero of the tale. Despite his earnest—and long-winded—attempts to put himself in the right, however, Victor's words only alienate us as they pile up. He feels little besides relief when the monster escapes; he lets Justine go to her death rather than risk his reputation by telling the truth; he whines and prevaricates; he heartlessly abandons and scorns his own creation. Ironically, Victor would be more appealing were he to lose the power of speech. Unlike his monster, he is no murderer. By themselves, his actions might seem reasonable. But because he bares his soul by communicating verbally to us, the readers, he reveals the unappealing motivations behind those reasonable actions and loses our trust and sympathy.

The monster's eloquent words do not have the effect he intends: They fail to win Victor's approval or gain his affection. They do have an effect he cannot foresee, however. By explicating himself and his actions, the monster gains our favor and turns himself into the hero of Victor Frankenstein's narrative. And by pulling off this neat reversal, Shelley demonstrates the overwhelming importance of language in shaping individuals' identities—as well as the perception of those identities by others.

GLOSSARY OF LITERARY TERMS

ANTAGONIST

The entity that acts to frustrate the goals of the *protagonist*. The antagonist is usually another *character* but may also be a non-human force.

ANTIHERO / ANTIHEROINE

A *protagonist* who is not admirable or who challenges notions of what should be considered admirable.

CHARACTER

A person, animal, or any other thing with a personality that appears in a *narrative*.

CLIMAX

The moment of greatest intensity in a text or the major turning point in the *plot*.

CONFLICT

The central struggle that moves the *plot* forward. The conflict can be the *protagonist*'s struggle against fate, nature, society, or another person.

FIRST-PERSON POINT OF VIEW

A literary style in which the *narrator* tells the story from his or her own *point of view* and refers to himself or herself as "I." The narrator may be an active participant in the story or just an observer.

HERO / HEROINE

The principal *character* in a literary work or *narrative*.

IMAGERY

Language that brings to mind sense-impressions, representing things that can be seen, smelled, heard, tasted, or touched.

MOTIF

A recurring idea, structure, contrast, or device that develops or informs the major *themes* of a work of literature.

NARRATIVE

A story.

NARRATOR

The person (sometimes a *character*) who tells a story; the *voice* assumed by the writer. The narrator and the author of the work of literature are not the same person.

PLOT

The arrangement of the events in a story, including the sequence in which they are told, the relative emphasis they are given, and the causal connections between events.

POINT OF VIEW

The *perspective* that a *narrative* takes toward the events it describes.

PROTAGONIST

The main *character* around whom the story revolves.

SETTING

The location of a *narrative* in time and space. Setting creates mood or atmosphere.

SUBPLOT

A secondary *plot* that is of less importance to the overall story but may serve as a point of contrast or comparison to the main plot.

SYMBOL

An object, *character,* figure, or color that is used to represent an abstract idea or concept. Unlike an *emblem,* a symbol may have different meanings in different contexts.

SYNTAX

The way the words in a piece of writing are put together to form lines, phrases, or clauses; the basic structure of a piece of writing.

THEME

A fundamental and universal idea explored in a literary work.

TONE

The author's attitude toward the subject or *characters* of a story or poem or toward the reader.

VOICE

An author's individual way of using language to reflect his or her own personality and attitudes. An author communicates voice through *tone, diction,* and *syntax.*

A Note on Plagiarism

Plagiarism—presenting someone else's work as your own—rears its ugly head in many forms. Many students know that copying text without citing it is unacceptable. But some don't realize that even if you're not quoting directly, but instead are paraphrasing or summarizing, *it is plagiarism* unless you cite the source.

Here are the most common forms of plagiarism:

- Using an author's phrases, sentences, or paragraphs without citing the source
- Paraphrasing an author's ideas without citing the source
- Passing off another student's work as your own

How do you steer clear of plagiarism? You should *always* acknowledge all words and ideas that aren't your own by using quotation marks around verbatim text or citations like footnotes and endnotes to note another writer's ideas. For more information on how to give credit when credit is due, ask your teacher for guidance or visit www.sparknotes.com.

LITERARY ANALYSIS

Review & Resources

Quiz

1. Who is convicted of the murder of Victor's younger brother, William?

    A. Alphonse Frankenstein
    B. Victor Frankenstein
    C. Justine Moritz
    D. Frankenstein's monster

2. Who is accused of the murder of Henry Clerval?

    A. Victor Frankenstein
    B. Robert Walton
    C. Frankenstein's monster
    D. Justine Moritz

3. To whom is Victor taken after Henry is murdered?

    A. M. Kempe
    B. His father
    C. Professor Waldman
    D. Mr. Kirwin

4. What is the name of the professor at Ingolstadt who first teaches Victor the methods of modern science?

    A. Krempe
    B. Clerval
    C. Waldman
    D. Beaufort

5. With what is Walton obsessed?

    A. Creating life
    B. Reaching the North Pole
    C. Finding a passage to the East
    D. Discovering the source of the Earth's magnetism

71

6. Where does Victor first have a conversation with his monster?

    A. In Victor's apartment in Ingolstadt
    B. In a field outside of Geneva
    C. On a desolate island off Scotland
    D. In a hut on a glacier near Montanvert

7. What does the monster want Victor to do to heal his loneliness?

    A. Create a female monster to be his companion
    B. Accept him into his family
    C. Destroy him
    D. Work to make him appear less hideous

8. How does Walton meet Victor?

    A. They work in the same laboratory on an island off Scotland.
    B. Walton escorts Victor northward in pursuit of the monster.
    C. Walton finds Victor on the northern ice and nurses him back to health.
    D. They are students together at Ingolstadt.

9. How does Victor's mother die?

    A. She drowns in a river.
    B. The monster strangles her.
    C. She catches scarlet fever from Elizabeth.
    D. She is executed for murdering William.

10. Who takes care of Victor when he falls ill after creating the monster?

    A. Elizabeth
    B. Henry
    C. Alphonse
    D. M. Waldman

11. How does the monster learn to speak? ✓

    Ⓐ By listening to Felix teach Safie his language
    B. By reading Victor's journal of his creation of the monster
    C. By learning from Victor
    D. He doesn't; he is born knowing how to speak.

12. To which character(s) in *Paradise Lost* does the monster compare himself?

    A. Adam and Eve
    B. Satan
    C̶. Adam
    Ⓓ Adam and Satan

13. Why does Victor accompany Henry Clerval on a voyage to England and Scotland?

    A. For entertainment
    B. To track down and destroy the monster
    Ⓒ To work on creating a female monster
    D̶ To study science

14. What does the monster think causes Felix, Agatha, and De Lacey to be unhappy?

    A. The death of De Lacey's wife
    B. The loss of Safie
    Ⓒ Poverty
    D̶ His own presence

15. Which of the following is not one of the alchemists whom Victor studies in his adolescence? ✓

    A. Cornelius Agrippa
    Ⓑ Lucretius
    C. Albertus Magnus
    D. Paracelsus

16. What do Elizabeth and Alphonse assume is the source of Victor's unhappiness?

     A.   Disappointment in his studies at Ingolstadt
     B.   Guilt about creating a monster
     C.   Grief over the death of Beaufort
     D.   Lack of desire to marry Elizabeth

17. How does Victor react to seeing Henry's corpse?

     A.   He has no reaction.
     B.   He denies that he is the murderer.
     C.   He cries.
     D.   He falls into a long, feverish illness.

18. To whom does Walton address his letters?

     A.   Victor Frankenstein
     B.   Margaret Saville
     C.   Elizabeth Lavenza
     D.   Justine Moritz

19. The Frankensteins' family home is in

     A.   Luxembourg
     B.   Geneva
     C.   Chamounix
     D.   Ingolstadt

20. Victor Frankenstein attends university in

     A.   Ingolstadt
     B.   Geneva
     C.   Edinburgh
     D.   Paris

21. Which of the following books is not one of those read by the monster?

     A.   *Paradise Lost*
     B.   *The Sorrows of Werter*
     C.   Plutarch's *Lives*
     D.   *The Inferno*

22. Why are Felix, Agatha, and De Lacey so poor?

    A. They were born poor.

    B. Safie's father stripped them of their fortune.

    C. The French court took their fortune and exiled them from France for helping Safie's father escape from prison.

    D. Felix spent the family's money courting Safie.

23. What is the monster's reward for saving a girl from drowning?

    A. He is shot.

    B. He is given a meal and a room and place to stay.

    C. He is beaten and chased away.

    D. He is cursed and ignored.

24. Why doesn't Victor protect his wife, Elizabeth, from the monster's attack on the night of their wedding?

    A. He does not think that the monster will come.

    B. He thinks that Elizabeth can protect herself.

    C. He misunderstands the monster's warning.

    D. He doesn't love Elizabeth anymore.

25. What does Walton do after Victor dies?

    A. He continues toward the North Pole.

    B. He remains stuck in the Arctic ice.

    C. He returns to England.

    D. He pursues Frankenstein's monster.

SUGGESTIONS FOR FURTHER READING

BANN, STEPHEN, ed. FRANKENSTEIN, *Creation, and Monstrosity.* London: Reaktion Books, 1994.

DONAWERTH, JANE. FRANKENSTEIN's *Daughters: Women Writing Science Fiction.* Syracuse: Syracuse University Press, 1997.

GLUT, DONALD F. *The Frankenstein Archive: Essays on the Monster, the Myth, the Movies, and More.* Jefferson, NC: McFarland & Company, Inc., 2002.

HOOBLER, DOROTHY and THOMAS HOOBLER. *The Monsters: Mary Shelley and the Curse of* FRANKENSTEIN. New York: Little, Brown and Co., 2006.

LEVINE, GEORGE, and U. C. KNOEPFLMACHER, eds. *The Endurance of* FRANKENSTEIN: *Essays on Mary Shelley's Novel.* Berkeley: University of California Press, 1982.

MARSHALL, TIM. *Murdering to Dissect: Grave-robbing,* FRANKENSTEIN, *and the Anatomy Literature.* Manchester and New York: Manchester University Press, 1995.